Crested Butte

Return to My Avalon

John L. Tezak

CEDAR HILL PUBLISHING

Crested Butte – Return to My Avalon

Copyright © 2005 John L. Tezak All Rights Reserved

No part of this book may be copied, duplicated, transferred, transmitted, reprinted or stored in a retrieval system by any means, electronic or mechanical, without the written permission of the copyright owner.

Book design and formatting by Rebecca Hayes

Cover design by Rebecca Hayes

First Edition Winter 2005

Published in the United States by
Cedar Hill Publishing
P.O. Box 905
Snowflake, Arizona 85937
http://www.cedarhillpublishing.com

ISBN 1-933324-00-7

Library of Congress Control Number 2005920868

Dedicated with Love to Mom & Dad

TABLE OF CONTENTS

PREFACE 1
ACKNOWLEDGMENTS 3
CHAPTER 1: FAMILY 5
CHAPTER 2: THE WAR YEARS 23
CHAPTER 3: INDUSTRY IN CRESTED BUTTE 31
   MINING 31
   COUNTY ROAD CONSTRUCTION 42
   RANCHING AND CATTLE PRODUCTION 55
   FUR TRADE AND OTHER FURRY TALES *57*
   TRAPPING 57
   MINK FARMING 58
   TAXIDERMY 61
   FURRY FRIENDS 62
   OTHER JOBS AND BUSINESSES *63*
   POLL TAX 63
   LOCAL BUSINESSES 64
CHAPTER 4: ENTERTAINMENT 67
   MOVIE THEATER 67
   MUSIC 68
   LODGES AND CLUBS 70
   HAPPY HOUR 71
CHAPTER 5: FISHING 73
CHAPTER 6: HUNTING 81
CHAPTER 7: SPORTS & GAMES 95
   MARBLES 95
   OTHER SUMMER FUN 98
   WINTER GAMES *100*
   SKIING 100
   SKATING 103
   SLEDDING 103
   TOBOGGANING 104
   CRUST WALKING 105

CHAPTER 8: THE MOST UNFORGETTABLE CHARACTERS 107
PEANUTS 107
OTHERS 109
CHAPTER 9: SCHOOL & CHURCH 115
SCHOOL 115
CHURCH 117
CHAPTER 10: HOLIDAYS 123
CHRISTMAS 123
EASTER 126
MAY DAY 127
MEMORIAL DAY 127
FOURTH OF JULY 128
HALLOWEEN 129
CHAPTER 11: OUR DAILY BREAD 131

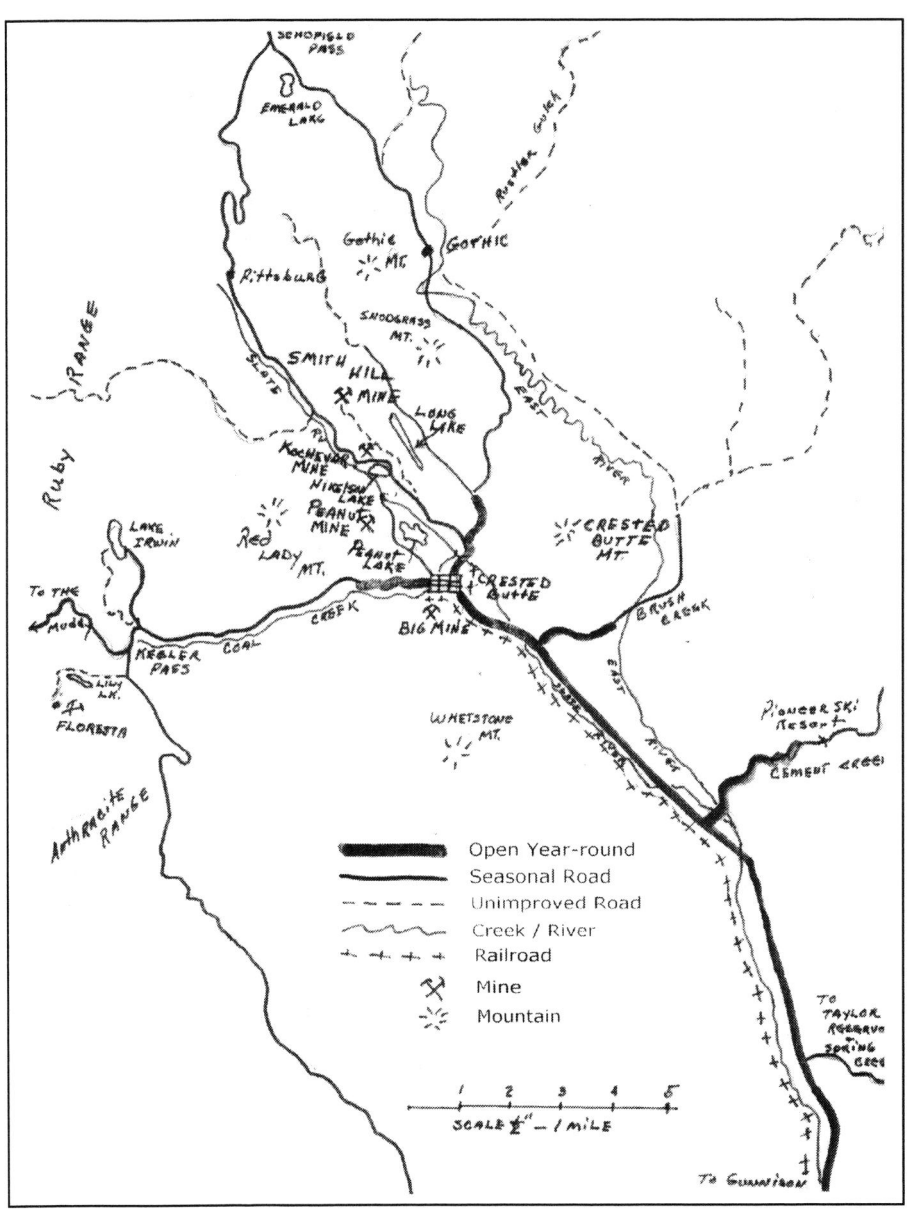

The story takes place here.

PREFACE

Mythical Avalon was a beautiful, enchanted island surrounded by a large, misty lake. It was to Avalon that Merlin took King Arthur to retrieve the sword, Excalibur. Excalibar was fashioned by an Avalonian elf smith with an unbreakable blade and life-protecting scabbard. This great weapon was presented to King Arthur by the Lady of the Lake. It was with Excalibur that Arthur fought the war against the Roman Empire and conquered most of Western Europe. He later carried Excalibur when he and his knights went on the quest for the Holy Grail, the cup of the Last Supper. The sword was stolen and King Arthur was mortally wounded in battle. His body was taken to Avalon, and Excalibur was subsequently recovered and returned to the Lady of the Lake.

My Avalon is not a mythical island. It is real, a beautiful town surrounded by majestic mountains. The mountains are covered with snow in the winter and resplendent with wild flowers in the summer. My Avalon is Crested Butte, Colorado.

In the late 1800's and early 1900's my ancestors arrived in Crested Butte from Slovenia. Their Excalibur was not a sword, but the picks, shovels and broadaxes, which became the predominant tools in the development of Crested Butte. Great Grandpa, Jake Kochevar, nicknamed Sem Djal, (meaning "I said," in Slovenian) arrived in Crested Butte in 1883. He was an explorer, prospector, and a builder. After several years in Crested Butte, he went back to Slovenia only to return with his wife and children. He and his son

Jacob built several buildings and bridges in Crested Butte, some of which are still in use today. Grandpa John Tezak arrived in Crested Butte in 1905. He was very glad to be in the United States and worked any job that was offered to him. The harder and the more dangerous the job, the more money it paid. His wife-to-be, Barbara Volk was promised to a flamboyant miner, gambler, and hunter, who paid her passage from Slovenia to Crested Butte. Instead, upon arrival in Crested Butte, she found her childhood sweetheart, John Tezak, and they were married. No one knows if the man who paid Grandma's passage ever got his money back. Grandpa John and Grandma Barbara moved to the mining camp of Floresta, Colorado where the winter's wrath blanketed the landscape with over twenty feet of snow. After four years and the birth of their first three children they settled in Crested Butte. There, Grandpa John became prominent in the Slovenian Lodges. He was well versed in the English language and was able to assist many of the local Slovenians with their letter writing, and showed them how to make money orders to send to their families.

This book is about the uniting of these two Slovenian families, and how they lived in my Avalon. It covers a time period from the late 1800's through the mid 1950's and is based on the stories that were told to me and stories that I remember when growing up in Crested Butte. Life was not easy, but being secluded in this valley, it was the only life we knew. Today we would be classified as living in poverty but then everyone's lifestyle was about the same, and we never knew we were poor. Everyone helped each other. We had family, love, food, drink and a tingle in our toes that made us want to dance at the first sound of a polka. This memoir is about that life: the families, romance, religion, work, hardship, activities and the vitality that comprised this period. Many of the people mentioned in this manuscript are no longer with us and now mainly rest in the Crested Butte cemetery. Mount Red Lady is their headstone and Mount Crested Butte, their footstone. The picks, shovels, and broadaxes they had used have been worn thin or rusted away. I wanted to capture a little of their lives. The mountains will remain unchanged. Some day, I too, will return to my Avalon.

ACKNOWLEDGMENTS

    I started *Return to My Avalon* several years ago while I was playing the part of caregiver for my Mom and Dad. When I got the chance, I would sit on the swing on the front porch and write and make notes about the stories they had told me. Mom was not much on remembering dates, but dad had a great memory bank. I wrote because I wanted to remember and record for others the wonderful stories they told. It, also, gave me a needed break from my many chores.
    After Mom and Dad passed away, I found I still had many holes about the early life in Crested Butte. On return trips to Colorado, I began to fill in the gaps after conversations with other family members. Uncle Martin "Teenie" Tezak, for one, loved to talk about growing up in Crested Butte. However I found that he also loved to add a little fiction to his stories, which I have since corrected.
    Uncle Bill Tezak was most informative and the most precise. He remembered everything and is quoted many times in the book. Without Uncle Bill, many stories about the family could not have been written. I spent two days with him and have several hours of our conversations on tape. Uncle Bill not only filled in some of the holes about the family but also was well versed in the building of roads in the Crested Butte Valley.
    Uncle John "Jonah" Spritzer and Aunt Ann were also very informative and the most fun to interview. Before arriving at their house, I always stopped at Safeway or a bakery and purchased a

banana cream pie. They loved banana cream pie, and it helped to sweeten our conversations. We would sit for hours discussing and recording stories of early Crested Butte. Uncle Jonah was my expert on the early music and coal mining. Having been in only the Kochevar Mine, he was able to tell me about the digging and delivery of coal from the big tunnel in the mountain to the tipple outside. Not only did Uncle Jonah tell me about mining; he acted out every word in his front room, demonstrating with his imaginary pick and shovel. I think we loaded several hundred ton of coal in this room. Not only did I listen to and tape many of these enjoyable conversations I was also entertained with music at the conclusion. Uncle Jonah would get out his accordion and play waltzes and polkas for me. After one session of conversations my sister Carol Ann arrived at the house, and as Uncle Jonah played his accordion, Carol Ann and I polkaed and stomped on the front room carpet for several tunes.

Speaking of sisters, both Carol Ann and Mary Rose (Mose) were my supporters while writing the book. Carol was my typist, spell checker, and critic. It was also Carol who kept me going. She was interested in every word I wrote, and with her positive attitude, she pushed me to completion. Her complements and encouragement prompted me to start and complete another chapter. Once I thought the book was complete, Mary Rose (Mose) volunteered to edit the manuscript. She corrected the spelling and sentence structure, but most valuable were the questions she asked. The answers required additional writing but made many of the sections more understandable. With all of the help I had from everyone, writing this book was fun and I actually felt a little despondent when it was completed.

Research about early Crested Butte by the end of this writing had become very difficult. Most of the "Old Timers", my main resources, have since passed away; Mom, Dad, Uncle Teenie, Uncle Bill, Uncle Jonah, and Aunt Ann. I feel so fortunate that I was able to spend time with them recording their history and to share a little part of their lives.

CHAPTER 1: FAMILY

The day Dad was born had to be a lovely day in late May. I can just imagine the setting; looking up through the tall pines at blue skies with some small fluffy clouds, the sun shining, spring flowers starting to bloom, and snow still in the shadows of the buildings and towering trees. One flaw, the snow is covered with coal dust. This event took place in 1908 at a coal-mining town called Floresta. (Spanish dictionary --- floresta n.f. glad, grove, beauty spot; anthology).

Dad was the first-born child of John Tezak and Barbara (Volk) Tezak, both immigrants from Slovenia. Uncle Martin (Teenie) Tezak has told several previous writers that Grandpa John and Grandma Barbara knew each other in Slovenia. Grandpa John's parents owned a grain mill in Radovici, Slovenia, and the Volk family from Radovica, a few miles away would bring their grain to the mill to have it ground. The mill was located on the north shore of the Kolpa River, which is the natural boundary of Slovenia and Croatia. The waters of the great Kolpa turned the large water wheel that powered the mill. A twelve-foot rock wall and the large concrete platform that provided the base for the Tezakva Mlin (Tezak Mill) are still standing.

The remains of the Tezak mill in Slovenia, in 2000.

Grandma Barbara was provided passage from Slovenia to Crested Butte with the intent of marriage to someone other than Grandpa John. That someone was John Plute. He was the hunter who had killed an elk that was recognized as a record by the Boone & Crocket Club. This recognition occurred several years after his death. The marriage never took place. Grandma Barbara married Grandpa John.

Floresta Breaker, in the early 1900's.

Floresta is located near the majestic Ruby Mountains and was previously called Ruby Anthracite. Its about ten and one half miles west of Crested Butte, or more specifically, in a valley just 2 1/2 miles southwest of Keble Pass. In the early 1900s the Floresta population was over 200 residents, and the coal mine was producing the highest quality of anthracite coal in the country. Today only broken timbers, mangled metal, and other debris, scattered on a large pile of coal slack as if destroyed by a bombing, are all that is left of the once largest coal breaker west of Pennsylvania. The only building still erect, but roofless, is a stone structure that was the grocery store, located near to where the coal breaker once stood. A hole, in the side of the mountain, beyond the valley, can be identified as the mine entrance. Between the mine and the coal breaker, are the log remains of some of the miners' cabins. The railroad bed, rails removed, can be identified off in the distance. Wild flowers now replace the steel rails.

The wages for working at the Floresta Mine were the highest in the area and the turnover rate of miners was also the highest. The working conditions were close to intolerable. The vein of anthracite coal was narrow and steep, and heavy gas concentrations were prevalent throughout the mine. The mining season was very short because the snows came early and lasted long into the spring. Over 25 feet of snow in these mountains was not unheard of, and this heavy snowfall made railroad travel impossible. Because of these conditions, the operation of the Floresta Mine lasted only slightly over 21 years.

Floresta Mine in the year 2000.

Living near the mining operations and the railroad in Floresta, Grandma feared Dad, who was quite young, would wander off. So to keep this from happening, she would tether him to the kitchen table with store string, (cotton twine, easily broken, used by butchers and merchants to secure the butcher paper around the wrapped meat). Grandma said that Dad would crawl to the end of the string, but he never broke it. This allowed her to take care of the other children and do the daily cooking and other chores.

Uncle Bill Tezak wrote about a trip he made to Floresta with Dad and Mom many years ago. The exact date of this trip is unknown, but it was in the early 1930s.

One Sunday, Carolyn, John, and I went to Floresta. The heavy winter snowfalls melted into the summer months, causing high swift water runoff. Eventually the Baldwin-Floresta crossroad was washed away, leaving large boulders exposed, making automobile travel impossible. So, at that time, hiking was the only way to get to Floresta. We opted to go to Floresta via the old railroad bed. Except for the three removed bridges, the railroad grade was quite level all the way to Floresta.

Floresta Mine, in 2000.

On the way we picked red raspberries, black currants, gooseberries, and red thimbleberries. Carolyn called the thimbleberries, sugar berries, because they were so fragile and sweet. Walking through the huge, solid stone cut at the last curve going to Floresta, John pointed out the waterfalls and a place called Chicago, which was only a small clearing north of Floresta.

What remains of Floresta Mine, in 2000.

In the ex-town of Floresta, we found fist-size lumps of anthracite coal mined there. John also pointed to the dilapidated, three-room house in which his parents lived and in which he, Mary, and Teenie were born. We exited Floresta on the road to Kebler Pass where John had parked the car. On the hillside across from Ruby Lake we found chanterelle and coral (cauliflower) mushrooms. John and I picked the larger mushrooms, but I noticed Carolyn picking the small, thumbnail size chanterelle. She called them button mushrooms and said that they were her favorites."

1930's ~ Rotary plow opening the railroad between Crested Butte and Gunnison.

In 1911 the Tezak family, now five --- Mary and Martin (Teenie) were also born in Floresta --- moved to Crested Butte. Grandpa John purchased a house on First Street, which remained the Tezak house until it was sold in the late 1980s. While in this house, seven additional children were born to Grandpa John and Grandma Barbara. The children were Frances, Cecelia, Barbara, Emma, Joe, William and Rose. Emma and Joe died in childbirth.

Dad had many vivid memories of his life in this house. He recalled the time that he and his Dad had purchased a milk cow and her calf. It was a very cold winter day and his Dad had borrowed a horse and sleigh from a neighbor, Mr. Malensek. His mother had dressed him in warm clothes. However, not having any warm boots of his own, she put her fur-lined boots on him for the trip. He remembers snuggling next to his dad during the all day trip to and from Mr. Guisieppo (Joe) Danni's ranch to make the transaction. The Danni ranch was about eight miles southeast of Crested Butte. On the following day, Mr. Danni's rider delivered the milk cow and calf.

Prior to modification by Grandpa John in 1911, both sides of the house looked the same.

Dad also remembers his father modifying the house. At one time he cut several feet off of the north side of the house for the total length of the house. He then added a coal, wood, and storage shed to the rear of the house, next to the alley. A covered porch was also constructed onto the north side of the house.

Dad was pretty much still "tied with a string" when he started school in the first grade. He had his many chores and was restricted from wandering too far from the house. As a result of these limitations, he entered the first grade not knowing a word of English. His family and friends only spoke Slovenian. Dad remembered his first teacher, Mrs. Long, and the many challenges. He said he always was good in math but didn't care much for the other subjects. One of his accomplishments was catching up with Fred Kochevar, Mom's brother, in the third grade. Fred started school two years before Dad but didn't like school and seldom went. He received most of his education hiding in Mrs. Scoy's yard or in the local icehouse.

Once Dad managed to break the string, his life changed. He no longer spent all of his time at home. He loved to fish, hunt, and swim and do all of the things growing boys in Crested Butte did. Uncle John Spritzer said that Dad knew all of the best fishing and swimming holes in the Crested Butte area and that he and several of the other boys were always trying to follow Dad to them. Uncle John said he got in trouble several times for following Dad after school instead of going home.

At age eight or nine, Dad had several chores to do. One of them was to feed and water the family's stock every morning. The animals were kept on a hillside pasture north of Saint Patrick Catholic Church. One morning when dad was walking to the pasture, he found a man lying on the hillside near the church. On closer examination he knew that the man was dead. Dad was really frightened. He forgot about his chores and ran home to tell his Mother about the man. The Tezak family had no idea that a murder had taken place, and that men on horseback were looking for the man dad had found.

The story as told by Uncle John Spritzer is as follows. The spelling of the names may not be correct.

"Mr. Joe Schaefer was a shoemaker and had his shoe repair shop in his home. His residence and business were located on Sopris Avenue between First and Second Streets. He was often harassed by some of the men in the community; one of whom was a man named Snyder. Mr. Schaefer took a gun to his shop, and when some men came by to harass him, he fired the gun several times. He killed a man named Henry O'Neal and another man. Curiously enough, the other man was not Snyder. Frightened, the shoemaker ran several blocks from his home and proceeded to shoot himself. He died near the Old Catholic Church where John found him. News of the murders spread wildly through the town." Uncle John remembers one of the men on horseback shouting, "Schaefer was found dead near the church, by that young Tezak boy."

(Research of notes I have from Dad and Uncle Bill, refer to the surname of the shoemaker as Schodich, not Schaefer.)

    A big change to the Tezak household took place on February 9, 1923.

    Grandpa John, slight of structure, big of heart, family man, passed away. Grandpa John died of complications from throat cancer at age 41. Dad, being the oldest, fifteen at the time, had to quit school and go to work. His first job was working at the Peanut Mine. It, like most mines, had a large working tunnel, where the coal was dug and removed. Parallel to the working tunnel was a second tunnel called the air tunnel, which provided air to the miners digging coal in the working tunnel. The two tunnels were connected every several hundred feet. There was a large door about 600 feet from the entrance to the working tunnel, which was only opened to let the mule drivers, mules and coal cars in and out of it. The door was closed immediately to trap the breathing air within the tunnel. It was opened and closed manually by a man entitled Trapper and was Dad's first job in the Peanut Mine. You might say Dad was the original Trapper John.

    At age 16, Dad started digging coal. The work of digging was much harder, but he could earn a lot more money doing it. Dad started in the Pershing Mine, but worked in all of the mines in and around Crested Butte. The experienced miners didn't want to work with Dad, because he was so young. They often called him *smrkavec,* (snot in Slovenian---snot-nosed kid.) Even though Dad preferred working alone, he remembered that his most steady digging partner was an old, Italian man named Quinto. As a digger, you were paid by the volume of coal you were able it dig and load into your coal cars. Since Dad was so young and working alone, the mule drivers, who came to pick up the cars and haul them to the tipple, would feel sorry for Dad and stop to help him load his cars before they would haul them off.

Dad worked winters in the coal mines and summers doing roadwork for the county. At the later his first job was rebuilding the road from the Crested Butte Cemetery to the town of Gothic. The roads at that time were built using teams of horses pulling scrapers. Mr. Malensek was Dad's job foreman at the time.

In June of 1926, Grandma Barbara married Lorenz Naglich. However their marriage was short-lived as Lorenz died in 1939. Grandma Barbara wrote the following letter to her daughter, Aunt Barie, on august 16, 1934. (Mom translated the letter.)

"My dear daughter Barie, I your Mother came from the old Country in 1907, 15 of March and I got married July 6, 1907. I had a nice married life with my husband. I was 25 years old. With my husband, your father, I lived 16 years. My dear husband, your father, died 1923. I tried to enlighten him with tears flowing from my eyes, but there was no help for him. I was a widow for three years and four months. I married again and got you a good stepfather that provided for care of you and me so that we could live.

Dear daughter Barie, I had to put up with a lot in this country and didn't know what was in store for me. From my heart, I wish all my children, especially you, joy and happiness like I had in this country for 53 years. For this my dear child, God give you joy and happiness wherever you go and whatever you do, never forget God. God, great God will never forget you for your happiness and health. This I wish for you. Your dear kind Mom."

Before Lorenz died the Tezak family, had to pack their bags and livestock and move west over Kebler Pass in search of work. Uncle Bill related the following.

"In August of 1928 the entire Tezak family, two cows, a dog and two cars moved to Bowie, Colorado, about 45 miles west of Crested Butte on Colorado Highway 135 in Delta county. John owned one of the cars - a topless, hoodless, and fenderless Model T Ford, name "The Bug."

One Spring day in 1929, John totaled the "The Bug" rolling over a steep bank. John, Teenie, and a friend were on their way to visit Uncle George Volk and his family living on a hay ranch at Ragged Mountain, more commonly known as "The Muddy." John was the only occupant seriously hurt in the flivver turnover. I remember seeing him lying in bed for a few days with a bandaged head."

The family was forced to move to Bowie because of the 1927-28 coal strike in the unionized coal mines in the United States, initiated by the Industrial Workers of the World-IWW. The strike devastated the town of Crested Butte and many of its inhabitants. Most of the men in Crested Butte were union members called, "THE WOBBLIES." The remainder, who refused to strike and were still working in the mine owned and operated by the C.F.&I, were called "SCABS." In Bowie, Lorenz Naglich, John and Teenie Tezak immediately found work in a non-union coal mine. Teenie, who was 17, worked as a "flunky" all around the outside of the mine and was paid $3.60 a day for an eight-hour shift.

Aunt Frances driving "The Bug", 1929.

Bowie had a school with grades one through eight only. Rosie started school in the first grade, Bill in the third, and Barie the seventh. Francy, a high school junior, and Celia, a freshman, rode the bus to Paonia High School, six miles away.

The family's move to Bowie in retrospect was a mistake as the strike was soon settled, and the men of Crested Butte went back to work. The Tezak family moved back to Crested Butte in August of 1929.

The biggest highlight of Dad's life happened sometime in 1927, at the Saturday night dance in the Croatian Hall. That was the night he met Mom, the beautiful, petite, dark haired Carolyn

Kochevar. Their two year courtship consisted of playing cards at each others homes with friends, long walks from town to the railroad depot and down the track, (they called this, a walk down lovers' lane), skiing parties, and picnics. Grandma Barbara, still with the store string, wrote Grandma Kochevar a letter questioning the proper chaperoning of Mom and Dad because Dad was staying out much later than the Tezak nine o'clock bedtime.

This courtship was inconvenienced twice. In the early fall of 1927 Dad became a student at the Coyne Electrical Engineering school in Chicago, where he studied basic electrical theory through the design and operations of complex generation systems. He graduated and received a diploma from Coyne in the spring of 1928 and returned to Crested Butte. Crested Butte was not the place for him to practice his newly acquired skills as many of the homes in Crested Butte didn't even have electric lights, so Dad returned to the coal mines. In the spring of 1929, the CF&I mine went on strike and Dad moved to Bowie to find work.

Even though the CF&I strike and subsequent move to Bowie inconvenienced their courtship, Dad made several trips back to Crested Butte and Mom and Frances Zakrasec went to visit Dad in Bowie in the summer of 1929. Dad moved back to Crested Butte before the rest of the Tezak family to repair the family home that had been rented and left in less than good condition. On November 16, 1929, Mom and Dad were married.

Mom's family history in Crested Butte goes back an additional generation. Great Grandpa Jacob Kochevar came to Crested Butte in late 1883. He was the first, or almost the first, of the immigrants from Slovenia to settle there. He left his wife Marija and four children in Slovenia, where he planned to return for them at a later date. Great Grandpa Jake was a prospector, a builder, and one of the early entrepreneurs of that time. Everyone who knew him called him Sem Djal ("I said," in Slovenian) because he preceded every sentence he spoke with "sem djal."

He would leave Crested Butte in early spring and sometimes not return until late fall. In those warmer months Sem Djal would be prospecting in the mountains for coal and mineral ores. He found and set claim to the Peanut Mine, Buckley Mine and others, only to lose all, because he refused to pay taxes. On his return to Crested Butte he lived in a boarding house located two doors west of the now Atrium

Garden Restaurant. It was actually both boarding house and brothel. It longer exists.

In 1888, Great Grandpa Jacob returned to Slovenia to bring wife Marija and children Jacob Steve, Mary, Katherine, and Anne back to Crested Butte. Jacob Steve, the oldest of the children, was 14 years old when he arrived in Crested Butte. Great Grandpa Jacob and Marija had two other children, Frances and Matthew, both born in Crested Butte.

In 1887, Great Grandpa Jacob and his son Jacob Steve started building. "The Big House" made of large hand hewn logs was completed in 1890. It is now Kochevar's Place and Karolina's Kitchen. Great Grandpa Jacob's original intention was to make this building living quarters with a bar and restaurant on the first floor, and a hotel and brothel on the second floor. The living quarters and bar were constructed and you can still see the partially completed doorways on the second floor but it was never completed.

The house on the left is Kochevar – "Big House"

Grandpa Jacob Steve married Rose Yaklich in 1901. The following year she and her baby died in childbirth. Shortly after Rose's death John Nemanic told Grandpa Jake Steve about a beautiful girl named Karolina in Leadville, Colorado. Karolina had recently arrived from Slovenia and was working as a waitress and a "dime-a-dance" girl at a bar owned by her sister Mary (Orazem) Terlip. Karolina was the "belle of the ball," and several miners were after her hand. Tall and handsome Grandpa Jacob Steve went to Leadville, won Karolina's hand, and they married in Leadville on June 30, 1902.

Grandpa Jacob Steve and Grandma Karolina lived in the Big House and raised a very large family. The children were, Rudolph, Fred, Mary (died at birth), Carolyn (Mom), Rose, Ann, Matthew, Josephine (JoAnn), Jacob, and Dorothy (Dotty). Great Grandpa Jacob and Great Grandma Marija moved to the Kochevar house two doors west of the Atrium. Jacob, who was rather unruly, and Marija finally separated and Jacob built and moved into a log cabin on Gibson's Slew on Chicken Ranch. Here Jacob raised the best cabbage, turnips, and other vegetables, and peddled them to the other residences of Crested Butte in an old wagon pulled by a small horse and a mule named Fannie. In his later years he moved to the log cabin behind the Big House (now the Soupcon) and resumed his prospecting and trapping. After he became ill, he moved into the Big House where his daughter-in-law Karolina tended to him. Great Grandpa Jacob died in the Big House in 1932. In the meantime, Great Grandma Marija had gone to live with her son Matthew in Pueblo, Colorado, and died in 1931.

Mom and Dad's first home after getting married was the little log cabin, behind the Big House, where Great Grandpa Jacob had lived.

I was born in the cabin on February 9, 1933, delivered by Dr. Stockdale, the C.F.&I. Mine doctor. Shortly afterwards, Mom, Dad, and I moved to the other Kochevar house located next to and west of the Atrium.

We lived there for several years. Soon after we moved in, Grandpa Jacob Steve plumbed it for cold water. Prior to this, cooking water was carried in from the Big House and water for washing clothes was taken from Coal Creek. The back rooms of the house were always rented to other families. Aunt Ann and Uncle John Spritzer lived there when they first got married.

On August 6, 1941, I had to share the love of Mom and Dad with my new sister Carol Ann. This was not difficult, as I loved my little sister very much. Carol Ann was born at the Gunnison Hospital. Everyone knew she was going to be a girl because, as the saying at the time went, "The highway between Crested Butte and Gunnison was very rough, a real washboard, and the trip by automobile would always shake the external plumbing off of all the new babies."

We left Crested Butte for about two years while Dad worked military construction during the early years of World War II but then returned to our same house and Dad to his work for the county in 1943. In the meanwhile, Dad with Grandpa Jake, and Grandpa Jake's sons, Rudy and Fred reopened the Kochevar Mine located on the hill north of Nickelson's Lake. It was worked weekends and evenings for a short while until failure to market the coal (slack) from the Kochevar Mine at a profit closed it again. Like all of the other coal mines in Crested Butte, it never reopened.

TOP LEFT: Writer and mother at the cabin where the writer was born. TOP RIGHT: Writer in a high-chair. BOTTOM: Writer and wife stand in the door of the restaurant that the cabin became.

During this stay in Crested Butte Carol Ann and I both shared our love of family with our new sister Mary Rose (Mose), who was born in the Gunnison Hospital on January 4, 1944. As was Carol Ann, Mose was a beautiful and much loved baby.

Kochevar Houses – sketch by Susan H. Anderton, 1971.

House on the right was a boarding house and brothel where Sem Djal lived, before building the Big House.

The house at left was where Dad and Mom and family lived from 1934-1944.

Later that same year, 1944, the John Tezak family left Crested Butte for good, only to return for visits and vacations. During one of these visits in 1945, I pleaded with Mom and Dad to let me remain in Crested Butte with Grandma and Grandpa Kochevar. Grandma sided with me and I was allowed to remain in Crested Butte for several months. During my stay there, Grandma and I had an agreement. I was to teach her to write in English and she in turn would teach me speak Slovenian. I'll never forget the day I helped Grandma address an envelope to Mom, which held the first letter in English that she had ever written. Grandma was so proud. I didn't do as well with my end of the agreement. I never really learned to speak Slovenian. I could pronounce all of the foods on the dinner table in Slovenian as, per our agreement, I could only have what I asked for in Slovenian. Grandma and Grandpa were not as strict as Mom and Dad and I realized a freedom and also responsibility that I never had before. I grew up during those few months.

On July 25, 1998, the Tezak and Kochevar families all met once again in Crested Butte. This time we came to bury the ashes and celebrate the lives of our parents, John and Carolyn Tezak in the Crested Butte Cemetery. Mom and Dad had returned to Avalon.

CHAPTER 2:
THE WAR YEARS

"Yesterday, December 7, 1941 --- a date which will live in infamy --- The United States was suddenly and deliberately attacked by naval and air forces of the Empire of Japan," President Franklin D. Roosevelt briefed Congress.

Congress declares war on Japan on December 11, 1941. On this same day, Adolph Hitler, the German Fuhrer declared war on the United States. Italy sided with Germany, and Britain formally declared war on Japan. The United States and Britain became allied powers in the largest war of modern time.

What did all of this mean to a nine year old boy living in Crested Butte, a town of only a few radios, less telephones, a weekly newspaper and the national news at the movie theater on Saturday night? The immediate impact was inconceivable. It was hard to believe that this new enemy was the same country that made the tin toys and the prizes in the CRACKER JACK box. The toys and prizes all said, "Made in Japan." Few people in Crested Butte even knew that Pearl Harbor was in the Hawaiian Islands.

The Japanese Admiral Isorku Yamamoto masterminded this surprise attack on Pearl Harbor and other islands in the Pacific. It was accomplished with 31 ships, 353 airplanes, and 5 midget submarines. 2403 Americans were killed and 1178 were wounded. Eighteen ships and 188 airplanes were destroyed or seriously damaged. After seeing these figures and the latest news at the movie on Saturday night, war became a reality to even a nine-year-old boy.

Almost overnight we heard unfamiliar words like draft, air raids, war bonds, and rationing. It wasn't long until we knew their meaning and that of many more new words and phrases all in the vernacular of war. In a very short time, every child in Crested Butte could identify every country in Europe and every island in the Pacific Ocean.

War became even more real when brothers, fathers, uncles, and other relatives and friends were called to fight. In Crested Butte, with a population of about 1,000, over 130 men and boys were drafted or volunteered for service of their country.

It wasn't long until many homes displayed a red, white, and blue flag in their windows with one of more stars indicating the number of family members in the service. Before the war ended, there were four homes whose flags displayed gold stars for *killed* or *missing in action*. The four gold star heroes from Crested Butte were Private First Class Albert Lee Manley, Technician Fourth Grade Louis P. Perko, Private First Class Frank L. Slogar, all killed in action; and William Savoren, lost in action.

Of the over 130 Servicemen, all were enlisted in rank. Only one became an officer. William V. Tezak, Uncle Bill, was drafted into the Army in 1942. While he was in training in California, an Officer asked if anyone could type and Uncle Bill after raising his hand was assigned as company clerk. During this assignment a request for Officer Candidates School (OCS) came across Uncle Bill's desk. He took it to his captain, who told him to put his name on the request and fill out the details. Bill was selected for OCS and upon completion was promoted to Second Lieutenant and sent to Europe.

While in Europe, Bill commanded an Anti-Aircraft gun company that saw active duty in France, Belgium, and Germany. He was the last officer of his company to leave Germany as the men with the most time in grade were the first to leave, and Bill had just been promoted to Captain. Uncle Bill left Europe in 1946 but this did not end Bill's military career; he was re-called by the Army during the Korean War.

I remember the many parties and dances when the heroes went to war, returned from leave, and most importantly, were discharged from the service. The family started the parties, in most cases, but the entire town would join in the celebrating. The largest were Victory over Europe (VE-Day), May 8, 1945, with the official signing of the surrender May 9, 1945, Victory over Japan (VJ-Day), August 15, 1945, and the official surrender of Japan on board the battleship "*Missouri*" in Tokyo Bay on September 2, 1945.

Uncle John Spritzer said that when he went to the Big Mine on August 15th 1945, all the miners were standing and sitting near the mine entrance. No one would work, as they heard the rumor that the war was over. Finally the mine superintendent announced that the war was indeed over. Hearing this announcement, the miners all went back to town. Uncle John got his accordion and many others joined him to play, march, and dance in the streets of town. The party lasted all day and through the night.

The war years were also difficult for the civilian populace, we who stayed at home. In the larger cities women worked in factories and defense plants. In Crested Butte, we didn't have defense plants or factories, but the women and the older and younger men were now responsible for many of the chores normally done by those now in the service.

Some of the older men became air raid wardens. Yes, air raids in Crested Butte. Not real raids, but the town was prepared. At some unannounced time, a few times a month during the early evening hours, the air raid siren would sound. Everyone was required to turn out all unnecessary lights, pull the window blinds closed and take shelter. The air raid wardens would patrol the streets and go door to door checking to see if everyone was all right and undercover. They would let you know if you hadn't pulled all of your blinds, and they could still see light shining through to the outside.

Savings became a way of life. We saved everything. We saved for the war effort, for a rainy day, and we even saved money in the form of War Bonds. War Bonds and stamps were bought at the Post Office and at school in ten-cent and 25-cent denominations until we could fill a stamp book with a value of $18.75. This book was exchanged for a war bond, which would mature in ten years to a value of $25. Bond drives were held at the school and on Main Street and "Buy Bonds" posters were everywhere. The coal miners were asked to have bonds deducted from their paycheck and to no ones surprise, these patriotic men contributed 100 per cent.

We who stayed at home soon learned the meaning of another new word --- rationing. Four days after the bombing of Pearl Harbor, the sale of new cars and tires was banned for civilians. Rubber was critical to the war effort, and the President called for a nationwide scrap drive. People turned in all old tires, garden hoses, overshoes, and other rubber products. This was just the beginning. To save rubber and gasoline, a national mandatory speed limit was established with a maximum speed of 35 miles per hour and gasoline rationing was implemented nationwide on December 1, 1942.

Gas rationing stamps

    There were several categories of gasoline rationing coupon books. The basic ones used for automobiles were the "A", "B", and "C" coupon books. Each vehicle had to display a windshield sticker showing the authorized ration under which each car was operating. An "A" coupon book was allowed for anyone who owned an automobile. It was established that moderate usage was necessary to keep engines and tires in good condition in case of an emergency. Therefore, an "A" coupon book allowed you to drive 150 miles a month. The supplemental "B" book allowed up to 470 miles per month including the 150 "A" book miles if the essential user could show that it was necessary to drive a greater distance to work. The supplemental "C" book was for doctors, defense workers, and clergy,

who could prove that it was necessary for them to drive over 470 miles per month. In order to maintain your ration books, tire inspections were required every four months and every two months for those with supplemental books. This inspection checked for proper inflation, serviceable brakes, rims and alignment. While driving to work you saw signs along the road reading, "*Is this trip necessary?*", "*When you ride ALONE, you ride with HITLER!*" or "*Join a car-sharing club TODAY!.*"
Gasoline and tire rationing was finally over by the end of 1945.

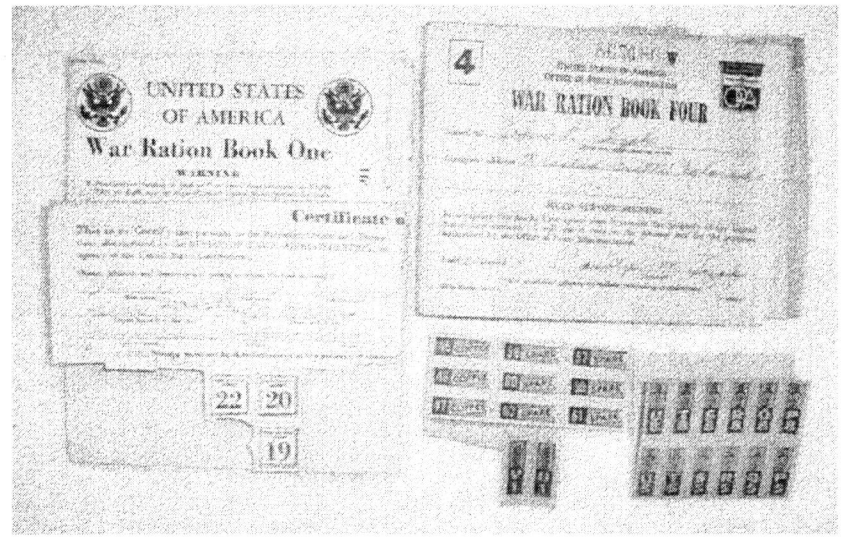

Food rationing stamps

Food rationing started with the rationing of sugar on May 2, 1942 and like gasoline and tires for automobiles, family members were issued ration books for food. Book I was used for sugar and coffee. Each individual was allowed one pound of sugar every two weeks and the housewife could apply for an additional five pounds each year for canning purposes. This sounds like a lot of sugar, but you couldn't buy pastries, candy, or cookies at the store so all were home-baked. Extra sugar was always the most sought after staple.

Coffee stamps in the ration books of children under the age of 15 had to be turned in. The coffee was equivalent to about one cup of coffee daily per adult. Second cups were usually made by adding a little fresh grounds to the already used grounds in the percolator. (I did the same thing when I was going to college, but it wasn't because I couldn't buy coffee in the grocery store.) Book II, which began distribution on January 1, 1943, was for processed foods. "Blue" stamps for vegetables and "Red" stamps for meat products. Each person was allowed 48 blue points and 64 red points per month. Some examples of stamp points were: butter, 16 red points per pound; canned applesauce, 25 blue points; grape juice, 20 blue points; pork chops, 7 red points per pound; condensed milk, 22 red points per can; and baby food, 1 blue point per jar. These point values changed from month to month, and it became necessary to post charts and to provide booklets showing customers how to get the most out of their ration coupons. Book III and Book IV were distributed at later dates and covered the items in books II and I when they were exhausted.

Fresh food in most cases, was not a problem in the smaller towns. We raised vegetables in the short growing season. Everyone had a "victory garden." The peddlers and farmers would come over Kebler Pass to sell fresh fruit and vegetables to us and we packed our cellars with fresh and home-canned vegetables and fruits. Many raised rabbits and chickens, and families might share a hog, which was made into hams and sausages and hung in the smokehouse. Most families took advantage of the hunting season, and deer and elk were canned and stored in the cellar as well. We could always depend on Uncle Fred for a fresh venison steak or roast during the winter months.

Shoes were also rationed but many items, even through not rationed were in short supply. Bicycles, typewriters, and lawn mowers were almost nonexistent, as were most metal and rubber products.

Store-bought cigarettes, "tailor-mades," were a luxury item and storekeepers kept them for themselves or friends when they did get them. Smokers would buy tobacco, paper, and a cigarette-rolling machine. Cousin John Michael and I rolled many a pack for his dad, Uncle John Spritzer. Odd brands of cigarettes showed up in the stores. One I remember was "*Wings*' that had an airplane card under the cellophane of each pack which we all collected. One of the advertisements of the 1940's was "*Lucky Strike Goes to War.*" Before the war the pack of Lucky Strikes used to be a dark green color with a red circle in the center. When green dye was needed army uniforms, Lucky Strikes changed from green to white.

Nylon stockings were only available for about a year when the war broke out. Women were so glad to get rid of the old, sagging, silk stockings, and they loved their nylons with the dark seam down the back. However, once the war began, nylon was needed for parachutes and nylons stockings became impossible to find. Even the saggy silk hose were unattainable as silk was also used in the war effort. Leg makeup was invented. I remember my aunts getting ready to go to a dance. They would apply a tan colored makeup to their shaven legs, and a sister or friend would draw a dark line down the back of the leg depicting the seam of the nylon stockings. The government also recommended that women diet, as there was no rubber for girdles.

Other fashion trends were also dictated by the war and rationing. Cotton and wool were used for uniforms, tents, bandages and other military items, therefore available to civilians in only limited supply. Men wore "victory shirts," narrow lapels, shorter jackets, and no vests or cuffs. Women's skirts ended one inch above the knee and all women's bathing suits were two-pieces.

Everything was recycled. Silk and nylon were recycled so that they could be made into ropes and parachutes. There were large scrap containers where we could deposit all metal and rubber products. Some of these containers displayed the slogan, "*Save your SCRAP, Kill a JAP.*" At that time toothpaste came in a soft metal tube. When we bought a new tube of toothpaste, we had to turn in our old rolled up one.

How many people today are aware that explosives can be made from kitchen fats? Fat makes glycerin and explosives can be made from glycerin. Women saved all of their kitchen fats and took them to the butcher where they were exchanged for two red ration points per pound of fat.

As kids growing up during this period, we made changes also. Every serviceman in town was our hero and when one would come home on leave, we would all go down town to see him. They wore their neatly pressed uniforms everywhere they went displaying their pride and patriotism. We knew every insignia and rank and collected all we could, wearing the insignia and stripes on our jackets and often a military cap given by a relative or friend to the school or church. Oh, yes, we did take caps off when we entered a building.

Our games changed. We now played war. We dug trenches and foxholes, and threw rocks for grenades. We always had an invisible enemy because no one would be one of the Axis.

Most of the boys built and collected ships, tanks, and airplanes. Airplanes were my favorite. I would spend hours building an airplane of balsa wood, sticks, paper, and glue, only to have it damaged in a wild crash.

The movies were also about war, and everyone looked forward to seeing the allies win another battle.

The war changed our lives in many ways. We learned about hardship, death of family members or friends, and as a town, we became very close, caring for each other and learning how to be self-sufficient. By war's end, we were experts in geography and the latest technology. We learned about new places like Hiroshima and Nagasaki, and things like Atomic Power. We also learned about its evils. World War II caused 15 million military personnel both, allied and axis, to be killed or missing in battle. Of these, over 295 thousand were Americans.

CHAPTER 3: INDUSTRY IN CRESTED BUTTE

MINING

It was mining of silver and other precious metals that established Crested Butte as a town in the late 1870's. Deposits of these metals were not found directly in Crested Butte, but in the nearby mountains. Like today, real estate depends on "location, location, and location." Crested Butte, ideally located at the junction of the Slate River and Coal Creek, could readily support and access the diggings at Gothic, Irwin, Washington Gulch, and other mines in the area. It seemed that almost overnight, Crested Butte had smelters, sawmills, hotels, stores, saloons, and other essentials to support the mines and miners.

During this same time period, another mineral was found --- coal, "Black Gold." It was located in every valley and mountain in and around Crested Butte. Both anthracite and bituminous coal were in abundance. The major mines that developed in the area were the Jokerville, Smith Hill, Floresta, Pueblo, Robinson, Pershing, Peanut, Buckley, Kochevar, and the Big Mine. When I lived in Crested Butte, only four mines were in operation; the Buckley Mine in 1940s,

Kochevar Mine in 1942 and 1943, the Big Mine until 1952, and the Peanut Mine operated on a part time basis only.

Local Mines:

ABOVE: Pershing Mine, 1920's. Photo purchased from Rijk's Family Gallery, Inc.

LEFT: Smith Hill Mine, late 1920's. Photo by Uncle Frank Sutey.

Kochevar Mine

RIGHT: Main mine shaft, 1943.

BELOW: Tipple destroyed by weather and snow. Photo taken in 1990.

The only active mine I ever entered was the Kochevar Mine. In 1942 it was reopened after having been closed in the early 1900's because there was little demand for slack. However, since coal (slack) was the basic ingredient for the new nylon and plastics needed for the war, there was a new and growing demand for it. The Kochevar Mine had anthracite coal in large lumps, which when removed from the mine and exposed to the outside air, broke into small pieces called "slack."

The Kochevar Mine is located on the mountain approximately one mile north of Nickleson's Lake. The old roadbed to the mine branched off of the Slate River road east of the lake and then northwest over the mountain to the Smith Hill Mine. A lower branch of this road went to the Kochevar Mine. Dad was working for the County at this time and reopened the road to the mine. He also built a new road from the Slate River road to the mine tipple.

As mentioned before, these were the war years, and labor was a problem. Uncle Matt and Uncle Jake Kochevar and the two Kikel boys, Matt and Mike, were in the service. Grandpa Jake and Mr. Mike Kikel built the tipple on weekends with the help of Dad, Uncle Fred and Uncle Rudy Kochevar. Uncle Jake Kochevar helped out the summer before he went into the service and I was at the mine when I wasn't in school.

One of my tasks was providing drinking water for the other workers. There was a small stream about 100 yards below the tipple, and I made the trip, carrying water, several times a day. I also spent a lot of time pulling and straightening rusty nails, which I had removed from a pile of old lumber that was later used in the construction of the mule barn and the tipple. I also found time to chase chipmunks and ground squirrels with my slingshot.

When the tipple was completed, Grandpa Jake worked on the mule barn, and Dad and the uncles worked the mine. There were two shafts into the mountain. The west shaft was the working tunnel, which unlike the large bituminous mines followed a small vein of coal. The ceiling and sides had to be shored up with large timbers to keep the mineshaft from caving in. This type of mining was slow, as they had to dig their tunnel through rock and dirt and shore it up as they progressed into the mountain. The narrow railroad from the tunnel went to the tipple and to a rock pile west of the tipple. I think the rock pile grew faster than the coal hopper on the tipple.

To work a mine like the Kochevar Mine, you had to be a Jack of all trades---a digger, a carpenter, and a muleskinner. You drilled your own holes, made your own dummy loads, and blasted the coal and rock in the mineshaft. You picked and shoveled the coal and shored the shaft, and when the coal car was full, you pulled it to the tipple with your mule. When the hopper on the tipple was full of slack, you loaded the dump truck and haul the slack to Crested Butte. The Denver & Rio Grande Railroad had a coal car on a side track southeast of town to transport the slack. I guess this was known as a one mule, one truck operation.

Whether using black powder or avoiding noxious gas you were completely responsible for your own safety. You made your own dummy loads at night. What are dummy loads? Dummy loads were made of newspaper wrapped around a broom handle to make a cylinder. The cylinder was filled with fine packed dirt or sand and crimped on both ends. After you had drilled several feet into the coal or rock, you would place your black powder cylinders into the hole, insert your fuse, and fill the remainder of the hole with firmly packed dummy loads. Without the dummy loads, the pressure from the ignited black powder would not penetrate the coal or rock but would only blow back out of the hole. The blasting of the coal and rock was usually done just before leaving the mine for the day. This allowed the dust to settle and the gas to escape before entering the mine the following day.

Coal miners, early 1900's. Note: Carbide lamps on helmets.

You didn't have battery-operated lamps for your hard hat, but used a carbide lamp that had an exposed flame and produced little light. Another bit of mining trivia is the miner's lunch bucket, which looked like a three-piece cylinder made of aluminum. It was about 8 inches in diameter and about 12 inches tall and made much like a double boiler used for cooking. The bottom of the three pieces was for your lunch and contained the handle. The upper container was use to hold your water and atop it was the lid. The lid had a small hole from which you could fill your carbide lamp with water or just use it for drinking. Grandpa Kochevar was not a drinking man, but he did enjoy a cool beer once in a while. After a hard day at the mine, he would hand me the bottom of his miner's bucket and a quarter. I would run down the street to Bill Starika's beer joint and have the bucket filled with beer. Bill always gave me a penny-candy treat, which was gone by the time I got home. Grandpa gave me the foam from the top of the beer. I always ran all the way home from Bill's as the foam evaporated pretty fast.

I remember other coal-related experiences. I recall helping cousin Leonard Tezak pick coal from under the tipple of the Big Mine after the mine had closed for the day. He would haul the coal home in four-wheeled kid's wagon. If we couldn't find coal under the tipple, we would climb into one of the coal cars near the tipple and throw out large lumps of coal in order to fill the wagon. I also helped Uncle Fred screen the slack piles at the Smith Hill Mine so that we could fill the coal shed with heating coal for the winter.

I have enjoyable memories of playing cops and robbers or war games at the old coke ovens, climbing the many covered steps to the top of the hill next to the Big Mine tipple, and taking a shower with Dad at the Big Mine on Saturday afternoons.

The following information about coal mining in Crested Butte was related to me by men who worked the mines. Dad and John Spritzer were my prime sources.

The Peanut Mine was an anthracite coal mine located northwest of Peanut Lake. It operated only part time in the 1930s and 1940s. Like the other anthracite coal mines in the area, it had only a small vein of coal about 24 inches high. Because the vein was small so also was the tunnel. This meant that the digger tunneled on his hands and knees and often crawled on his belly using shovels and picks with handles they had shortened to dig the coal. These small tunnels were several feet from the main tunnel, and the digger would have to move the coal several times to get to the main tunnel where he could load the coal car.

In the early 1920s, when the Peanut Mine was in full operation, an investor visiting Charles L. Ross, owner and general manager of the mine, questioned a very large paycheck a miner named Fred (Fritz) Kochevar had received. The investor wanted to meet this "big guy" who could load over 25 tons of coal in one day. He was amazed when he shook the callused hand of the little redhead, who weighed less than 120 pounds and understood why Uncle Fritz was given the nickname, Little Dynamite.

The Buckley Mine was a bituminous coal mine located about two miles southeast of Crested Butte. Coal was plentiful at the Buckley Mine, but the mine itself was operated under great hardships. It was located in an avalanche area and was destroyed several times by snow slides. Because of the snow slides, the coal miners all lived in Crested Butte. Going to and coming from work was difficult, as the miners had to either walk or ride on horseback. Many days during the winter, they took turns breaking a trail to and from work. Dad worked the Buckley mine in the mid-1930s. John Spritzer was a delivery boy for the John Bayuk Store and remembered delivering oats in 25 pound bags to Dad so that he could feed his transportation to and from the mine. The Buckley Mine closed in the mid-1940s.

The Big Mine, which operated from 1894 until 1952, was owned by the Colorado Fuel and Iron Corporation (CF&I). It was located on the south side of Crested Butte on the Gibson Ridge. This mine was the major source of income for the people of Crested Butte for many years. In the early 1940s, it employed over 350 men and the average production of coal was almost 2,000 ton per day with a two-shift operation.

The CF&I not only owned the mine, it almost seemed like it owned all of the people in the town of Crested Butte. It owned company housing which was rented to the miners, the Company Store, which provided both food and mercantile, and a company service station across the street from the Company Store. In fact, the only doctor in town was an employee of the CF&I. Credit was a way of life, and "payday," in many cases, became "break even day." Competition and credit from the other merchants in town was the only thing that kept you from, "owing your soul to the Company Store."

Employee and company ties were not strong when I was growing up in Crested Butte. After the CF&I signed a contract with the United MineWorkers (UMI) in 1933, working conditions at the mine and living conditions for the miners and their families improved. The threat of losing your job if you didn't vote the way the company wanted you to, or if you didn't do all of your business at the Company Store was no longer standard practice. John L. Lewis became a person of high regard. In fact, the miners worshipped God and John L Lewis. I think in that order. He was the president of the United MineWorkers' Union.

CF&I – "Big Mine"
Late 1940's

Upper picture purchased from Rijk's Family Gallery.

ABOVE: Company store. BELOW: Company gas station.

The townspeople of Crested Butte were also controlled by bells and whistles. The whistle at the Big Mine sounded several times a day telling you when to start work, when to have lunch, and when to quit work. The last whistle of the day even told you whether or not the mine would be in operation the following day. One long blast--work tomorrow; two short blasts---no work tomorrow. The townspeople didn't need to carry a watch, but those did always took it out of their pocket to see if the whistle was on time. If the whistle ever sounded at anytime other than its normal scheduled times, everyone became silent and prayed. This unscheduled whistle meant that an accident had happened at the mine.

Besides the mine whistle we had a large bell hanging in the City Hall that also had more than one purpose. Every night it rang eight times, at eight o'clock, reminding all of the kids that it was curfew and they had better get off the streets and into their homes. It also rang unscheduled if there was a fire in town. A siren replaced the old bell in the late 1930s or early 1940s. The siren had an additional purpose. It sounded to report an air raid or practice air raids during World War II.

Uncle John Spritzer related the following story of a typical day for a digger in the Big Mine.

You get up in the morning, have a large breakfast, and head toward the mine. It was still dark out. Once you got to the base of the tipple, you walked the many steps up the hill and continued on to the bathhouse. At the bathhouse, you changed into your mining clothes. There were no lockers in the bathhouse. Each miner had a long chain on a pulley hanging from a very high ceiling. He would unlock his chain, reel down his mining clothes, hook up his street clothes, reel them to the ceiling, and lock his chain. The bathhouse was always warm and your clothes were always dry when you put them on. After dressing for the mine, you went to the lamp room and picked up your lamp and your brass identification checks. Then you went to the mule barn, harnessed your mule and walked to the mine entrance. It was usually still dark outside. You walk leading your mule about two miles into the mine. Once you arrived at your entry tunnel, you'd hitch your mule to an empty two ton coal car and proceed another mile further into the mine. There you'd find your partner, mine was Frank Slogar, cleaning the area and loading an empty car with coal."

Unlike the Peanut Mine, where you often worked in a small area, lying on your side, the Big Mine had large veins of bituminous coal, some over 20 feet high. In this working tunnel, the miners cut rooms into the coal and left large pillars between each room that supported the ceiling so that minimal shoring with logs was necessary. Every 50 feet into the tunnel, the miners would dig a crosscut entry to the air tunnel. In the entrance of the air tunnel was a large fan that forced outside air into the tunnel to provide air for the miners. John Spritzer's father was responsible for keeping this fan lubricated. Back to Uncle John's story.

"After greeting your partner, you would help load the coal car. First you shoveled the coal into the car and then you topped it off with large lumps of coal. Proper loading was necessary as the car traveled at a high speed on its final leg to the tipple. When the car was loaded placing your brass check on the nail on the side of it properly identified it. Your partner and you would take turns hanging your brass identity checks on the side of the loaded car as you both had different identity numbers. You now hooked your mule to the car and pulled it to the first park. This park was called a "parting." You would disconnect your mule from the full car, hook onto an empty car and return to your working area. When you had seven or eight cars at the parting area, you would turn on a small light. This signaled the mule skinner with a team of three or four mules to bring you empty cars and pull the seven or eight filled cars to the main line."

(Charlie Niccoli and John Merritt were muleskinners. Dad was also a muleskinner when he worked in the Big Mine).

"At the main line, 15 cars would be hooked to a steam powered wench and pulled to the tipple at a very high speed in excess of 60 miles per hour. At the tipple, the cars were weighed, the brass identification check was removed, and the miner given credit for the load. The load was usually between 4000 and 4500 pounds."

While all of this movement was taking place, the digger was still loading cars, which was not his only task. It was just the only task for which he was paid. In order to get to the coal the diggers had to shore the ceiling when necessary, lay track to the digging, and remove the track before the blasting with black powder would take place.

The digger did not shoot the black powder but was responsible for drilling and setting it. He would usually take 16 sticks of black powder with him to the work site and before leaving for the day, would drill six to eight deep holes into the coal, placing about 2 1/2 sticks of black powder into each of them. After inserting fuses, he would tamp about six dummy loads into each hole behind the black powder. During the evening, after the digger had left for home a powder man would shoot the powder. George Krismanich was John Spritzer's powder man. This night-shift crew would use electric machines to undercut the coal several feet back, under the bottom of the coal seam, and then fire the black powder charges. Undercutting permitted the coal to break up more easily when the explosive was discharged. In the morning when the digger returned, the coal was ready to load.

In a good day, Uncle John and his partner could load and deliver 18 to 20 cars of coal. The going rate paid was ninety cents a ton. As mentioned earlier in this chapter, each car held between 4000 and 45000 pounds of coal, an average of over two tons per coal car. With a going rate Uncle John and his partner would each average about 18 to 20 dollars per day. A digger with a good room made more money than muleskinners and other mineworkers. The going wage for the other mineworkers was about 8 dollars per day.

After a hard day of digging, Uncle John and his partner still had a three-mile walk out of the mine. They'd take their mules to the barn and looked forward to a hot shower. All clean and dressed, it was almost time for dinner. Maybe there would be time for a quick shot and a beer at Tony's before they'd go home. It sure is cold and dark outside.

COUNTY ROAD CONSTRUCTION

The County of Gunnison under County Commissioner Bill Whelan, was in charge of all road construction and maintenance in the mid-1930s and 40s in Crested Butte. There were no private contractors. The new County garage was built on Fourth and Elk avenues housed all of the road equipment that consisted of a 30 Caterpillar, a 60 Caterpillar, a non-powered grader, dump trucks and a pickup truck. A new red International bulldozer was also purchased in the late 1930s. The 30 Cat was actually built by the Holt and Best Company, which merged with Caterpillar in the early 1930s. It was used primarily to pull the road grader and had a semi-fixed dozer blade that was hand built by Dad and others from an old steam boiler discarded by the C.F.&I. mine.

Road construction was seasonal, but maintenance and cleanup were year round. During the summer the County employed several construction workers but in the winter months cut back to only one or two. Dad became a fulltime employee during the summer of 1935.

During the winter months Dad would start work early in the morning and quit late at night. Most of his time was spent on the bulldozer plowing snow and primarily keeping the road open to Gunnison. After a snowstorm it was not unheard of to experience 12-foot drifts on the highway. Once the road to Gunnison was open Dad would start on the streets in Crested Butte, and the roads to the city dump and to the cemetery. Plowing snow in and around Crested Butte could start as early as September and sometimes not end until March. When Dad wasn't busy plowing snow, he spent his time servicing the equipment in the garage. There would be little time for maintenance during the short summer construction period.

1938 – Highway 135 between Gunnison and Crested Butte.

  As early as age three, I would spend many days riding with Dad on the bulldozer as he bucked the snow in and around Crested Butte. Mom would fix lunch for both Dad and me, bundle me up in my snowsuit and overboots and give me a big hug. Then Dad would carry me to the huge bulldozer and lift me up to the top of the tracks where I'd wait until Dad climbed up the other side of the dozer and opened the door. I then crawled onto the big seat in the cab next to him and we were off. I would wave at my friends as we bucked snow around town. In fact, I would wave at everyone. It was a great feeling to be on the big bulldozer with Dad and I was the envy of every kid in town.

1936 First Bulldozer and Snow Plow.

John L. Tezak, Sr. & Jr.

The writer and his dad in 1936.

When spring came and the snow was melting, other cleanup tasks were required and extra men hired to work through the summer. Mr. Whelan told Dad that he expected the road over Kebler pass to be opened every year for Memorial Day. Some years the snow was still over 12 feet high on the pass. The snow was pushed with the bulldozer over the side of the mountain into the canyons except near the top where in the absence of canyons it had to be hauled and sometimes hand shoveled. Dad said that there were some years when opening the Kebler Pass seemed impossible, but he always seemed to manage it by Memorial Day.

When the snow melted, all the roads were in very poor condition, with large chuckholes, a washboard surface, and very little gravel left. First reconstruction started near Gunnison and went north on the Gunnison to Crested Butte highway. The road grader was hooked to the 30 Cat and towed up the road. John Perko was the grader man, and Dad drove the 30 Caterpillar. Two men walked behind the grader with manure forks and picked up and tossed the larger rocks to the side of the road. When the surface was scraped and the chuckholes and washboard removed, gravel was spread on the newly graded surface.

Snow of 1938 in Crested Butte.

When the road between Gunnison and Crested Butte was completed, all of the streets in Crested Butte were resurfaced in the same manner. The crew then continued the task up Elk Avenue and over Kebler Pass. The roads to Pittsburg, Gothic, and Emerald Lake had to be resurfaced. Many of these roads were not completed until summer as they were probably the recipient of a winter avalanche, covering them with snow, ice, trees, dirt, and rock. Once all the roads were open to traffic, it was time to start new construction.

Kebler Pass, 1938.

ABOVE RIGHT: Mr. & Mrs. John Lloyd, Miss Eppich, and Miss Faberburg ~ the first car over Kebler Pass. 1938

BELOW RIGHT: Hand-shoveled gothic road, 1934.

Dad's first job as a full time employee in 1935 was rebuilding the road from Crested Butte over Kebler Pass. Many of the sharp curves were removed, and the road was totally reconstructed on the old railroad bed. Dad was the overseer of the job and had to keep labor records for each man, whose rate of pay was $3.50 a day. Early every morning at the County shop Dad's crew would pile onto the bed of his pickup truck and they would drive to the job. Usually on a Monday morning, Johnny Perko would crawl into the rear of the pickup with a super hangover. As soon as the truck started up the hill, he would take out a large white onion from the lunch his Mother had prepared for him and eat the whole thing. Dad said, "He ate it just like you would eat an apple. After he finished the onion, his hangover was gone, and everyone in the back of the truck had tears in their eyes."

As long as we are picking on Johnny Perko, the following is another story related by Dad.

"When you started the 60 Caterpillar you had to prime each cylinder, turn the flywheel to top dead center, turn on the ignition, and then turn the flywheel sharply with a long pry bar. The flywheel was turned and the bar removed in one sequence. If not done properly, the flywheel could kick the bar upon starting and injure the operator. One time, Johnny Perko held on to the long heavy bar too long, and when the flywheel turned, it threw him several feet into the air, and over the hood of the Caterpillar. Johnny was sore and bruised but had no broken bones."

Dad also had his own bad experience while starting the 60 Caterpillar. During the start cycle, Dad released the long pry bar. It kicked backwards and caught Dad on the wrist. He wasn't thrown over the Caterpillar, but he spent several months with his left arm in a cast with a broken wrist.

The following summer, one of the construction projects was rebuilding sections of the road from Crested Butte to Gothic and north of Gothic to Emerald Lake. The large hill and curve north of the cemetery was widened, and by removing a portion of the hill, the sharpness of the curve was reduced. Larger culverts were installed under the road. I think this was also the year that the County crew replaced the old trestle bridge across the Slate River, near the cemetery with a bridge made from the old turntable from the Smith

Hill Mine. The turntable was dragged to its Slate River location from the mine by one of the Caterpillars.

Much of the following story is taken from Uncle Bill Tezak's recorded notes.

"In 1937 John was in charge of the rework of large sections of the highway from Crested Butte to Gunnison. Prior to this date, the highway made several 90-degree curves, and followed the boundaries of the ranches in the area. The County purchased the right-of-way from several of the ranchers and began to remove many of these hazardous curves. Two of the 90-degree curves were the boundary of the Sampson Ranch and were called the Sampson curves. During the same summer, the road was reworked over Comstock Hill, and a roadbed was made across the lake just north of it. Comstock Hill is located just east of the Roaring Judy Fish Hatchery. Prior to the rerouting, the road made a sharp curve around the eastside of the lake."

Uncle Bill was hired by Dad to work with the construction crew when he was 17 years old. Every morning Dad would meet Uncle Bill, Bill Nelson, and John Skoff and drive to the job site. Uncle Bill said he had several jobs during the day. He was a flagman, helped build fences, and helped Dad grease all of the equipment every evening before quitting time. The large amount of rock on Comstock Hill required a lot of blasting with dynamite. Dad operated the bulldozer, Tom McCartney was the steamshovel operator and Uncle Bill, as the flagman, was responsible for stopping traffic until the road was made passable again.

Another major change to the highway was completed by Dad and his crew just north of the ranch owned by Sid Nicolli, possibly around the same time as the work on Comstock Hill. The original road crossed the river, made a sharp turn and then ran adjacent to the Glacier Schoolhouse. Dad was responsible for straightening the road and building a new bridge across the river.

Uncle Bill said that this was not the first job that he had with the county. The previous year he was hired to be a vehicle counter. Road usage by vehicle traffic is the method used by the county to justify future money for road repairs and in enhancements. Today you don't hire an Uncle Bill to count vehicle traffic. An electronic counter does it. We have all run our cars over an electronic, pressure sensitive cable that looks like a black rubber garden hose stretched across a road which sends a signal to a box counter each time it is run over. Uncle Bill was responsible for counting all of the vehicles travelling on the Gothic Road, in an eight-hour period over several weeks time. He established his lookout and position on a hillside near the road where the ski resort now sits. In 1936 there probably weren't over 20 or 30 vehicles owned by the total population of Crested Butte. Uncle Bill found this to be a very boring job and the time passed very slowly. He made a study of the many ants and other insects and became an expert on the different flowers and plants in the area. There were days when he didn't need his tally board. He could count all of the cars on his fingers. To pass the time of day, he also built a checkerboard and often his friends would walk up the road to challenge him to a game. The results of Uncle Bill's count was sufficient however to establish funds for repair of the road later in the summer and major enhancements the following years.

During the summer of 1938, Dad with his construction crew rebuilt the road from Emerald Lake, over Scofield Pass, through Crystal Canyon, and into the town of Crystal. For this job, the workers actually lived at the construction site during the week, returning to Crested Butte on weekends. The workers lived in a large boarding house previously inhabited by the Ajax Mining Company. The main floor had a kitchen, living room, and a large dining room. The second floor had one bedroom in which Dad and Grandpa Kochevear slept and a second room, which was a large open bay with cots and beds for the other workers. Apart from the main house there was a small cabin where Mrs. Kate Sigman and Mrs. Valine, who were hired as cooks, lived.

Uncle Bill remembered that Dad, Bill Nelson, Grandpa Jake Kochevar, Martin Slobodnick, Esko Long, Roy Tenike, Theodore Valine, Mr. Ackerman, and Uncle Bill all lived at Ajax House while working on the road. When Uncle Bill left for college, Uncle Matt Kochevar took his place. Dad said that Billy Dunn, Joe Saya, and the Campbell boys were also there at different times. I spent a week with Dad at the construction site, but being only five years old, I wasn't on the payroll. I think the two things I remember best about my week with Dad at Scofield and living at the Ajax boarding house were the biscuits made by Mrs. Sigman and the large stack of comic books Billy Nelson let me look at every evening.

(My apologies if the spelling of any of the surnames is not correct.)

Constructing this road was a monumental task. It required cutting a road through almost solid rock on the side of a steep mountain and erecting two log bridges across the Crystal River. One of the bridges was in a clearing near the top of the pass, and the other was at the river crossing below The Devil's Punch Bowl.

Rebuilding the road from Emerald Lake to Crystal, 1938. Scofield Pass and Devil's Punchbowl.
BELOW: Devil's Punchbowl.

The Devil's Punch Bowl is a large pool of water in a crater, at the bottom of a waterfall on the Crystal River. A steep road runs along the side of the crater. Stories are told of people and their transportation falling into the crater and never being recovered. Dad told me that at one moment in his life, he thought he would be one of those lost souls. He was cleaning recently dynamited rock from the road surface with the Bulldozer, when he got too near the edge. The big dozer was teetering on its track and Dad didn't know what to do. He considered jumping free of the dozer before it plunged into the crater. Instead he gently placed the bulldozer in reverse and the big machine crept back onto solid ground. Once safe he got down off the bulldozer. He sat on a large rock and watched the clouds roll by for some time before he went back to work.

Esko Long and Ackerman were the dynamite men. While they were drilling and blasting the rock on the roadbed, Dad and Theodore Valine were dragging long logs to the areas where the bridges were to be built. Dad said that the bulldozers were limited at these high altitudes. Their engines were starving for air and they lost so much power that they could hardly pull their own weight.

I rode my motorcycle over Scofield Pass into Crystal in 1978. During that trip, while riding up the solid rock roadbed adjacent to the Devil's Punch Bowl, I saw several holes that had been drilled in the rock roadbed but were obviously never filled with dynamite or exploded. The holes were filled with wooden plugs. You can still find drill holes on the rock pass that for some reason were never shot.

The bridge builders were Grandpa Jake Kochevar and Roy Tenike with several men helping them. Grandpa Jake carried three axes---one for heavy work such as cutting branches, one for cutting notches, and his huge broad axe for hewing the long large logs. He would stop often to put the whetstone that he carried in his back pocket to one of the axes, as they were all kept razor-sharp. Once the branches were trimmed from the large tree trunk, this log was held steady with large chains. Grandpa Jake would tack a chalk line to both ends of it and then go to the middle of the log, pick up the taut chalk line and snap it sharply leaving a straight blue chalk mark the length of the log. With his notching axe, he would cut a notch every so many feet from the bark of the log to the chalk mark and square the log along the chalk mark to the first notch. He would continue hewing the log from notch to notch along the chalk mark with his broadax until the complete side of the log was squared. When Grandpa finished the log, it was as straight as if cut with a power saw. Uncle Bill said, "I really admired him. Of all the workers on the job, your Granddad was the best. Boy, he was good at his job with the broadax."

Dad told me another story about splitting a log. I don't think this happened on the job at Scofield Pass, but at another site. "Roy Tenike was cross-eyed and was in the process of splitting a log. He had Joe Saya holding the wedge for him as he prepared to strike the wedge with his heavy maul. Joe stretched his arm as far as he could and still hold onto the wedge. He looked up at Roy and said, 'Are you going to hit where I am holding or are going to hit where you are looking?' Everyone including Roy rolled over in laughter."

The road and bridges at Scofield Pass were completed before the first snowfall. However an avalanche destroyed the upper bridge the following winter. I don't think the pass was ever opened again to automobile traffic. I made the trip from Emerald Lake to Marble over Scofield Pass with an off road motorcycle the summer of 1979.

In the summer of 1939, Dad took a small crew of workers to Ragged Mountain to rebuild a portion of the road on the East fork of the Muddy River. This site was about 50 miles from Crested Butte but in 1939, this distance was a two to three hour drive. Dad rented a cabin at the Muddy that belonged to a rancher named Charlie Ray and Mom, Dad, Uncle Jake, and I piled into the old County pickup with some dishes, extra clothes and linens that Mom had packed and we headed West over Kebler Pass to the Muddy. I don't remember much about the road construction, but even though over 60 years have gone by the wonderful memories are vivid in my mind and I always smile when I reminisce about the things that happened while we were living there.

The cabin, made of logs, had a front room, a small kitchen, and a bedroom. It didn't have running water but we carried water from a well located across the road at Mr. Ray's large ranch house and the toilet was an outhouse located several yards to the rear of the cabin. On the second day that we were there Jake and I had to investigate a large haystack located across a barbed wire fence, not far from our cabin. We found that with some effort, we could climb to the top of it and slide to the ground. We also found that jumping up and down in the middle of the stack was great fun. The thing we didn't know until that evening was that, playing on a haystack was not a good thing to do. That evening Mr. Ray came over to talk to Dad. Much to their consternation they had to rebuild the haystack with pitchforks. We didn't play on the haystack anymore.

1939 – Uncle Jake and the writer at Muddy.

  The first week we were at the Muddy, Mom and Dad decided we could visit friends and relatives. On Sunday, we could travel to see the Valines, have lunch with Uncle George Volk and family, and then we could go and see the Bears. Things worked out pretty much as planned. We visited the Valine family, had lunch with our relatives, the Volks, and then we went to visit a family named Medved. As we left the Medved's Dad stopped along the side of the road, and we all got out of the truck to pick wild gooseberries that were ripe, and plentiful. We filled a large bucket with the ripe berries looking forward to Mom's gooseberry pie and then Dad said it was time to go as it would be dark soon. I asked Dad, "When are we going to see the bears?" Dad said, "We already did!" I didn't know that Medved was the word for bear in Slovenian.

One day Mr. Ray brought Mom a freshly killed chicken and I'll never forget the dinner she prepared. She fixed homemade chicken noodle soup, which was not new to our family, but this recipe was different. Mom plucked the feathers, dressed the chicken, cut it into pieces, and put it in a large pot to boil. After the chicken had boiled for a period of time, Mom removed the feet-- yes, the feet of the chicken from the pot. When the feet had cooled to the touch, Mom removed the transparent skin covering them and then removed the toenails. She then put the skinned feet back into the pot to continue cooking with the rest of the chicken. I wanted the toenails and Mom let me have them. I kept them in an empty Aspergum box for several years. I remember that the feet, after being boiled turned in a deep yellow color. When the soup was ready to eat I don't know how we divided the two feet, as there were four of us but I think we all got to nibble on them. I can't remember what they tasted like, but if they tasted anything like her chicken soup, they had to be good. This was the first and only time I can remember Mom cooking the feet of a chicken. I had eaten her delicious chicken soup with hand cut noodles for many years before and after the Muddy.

Mr. Ray had to leave the ranch for a few days, and he had asked Dad if he would tend to the stock while he was gone. I went with him every evening to feed and water the stock, the chickens and ducks, and milk a couple of cows. I enjoyed helping to feed all of animals but last came the other chore---milking. Dad had a bucket of warm water and soap, which he used to wash the udders. Then he rubbed them with a salve, a Vaseline- type substance, and placed a clean bucket under the cow. He sat on a three-legged stool, which he placed on the left rear side of the cow and started milking. For someone who hadn't milked a cow in many years, he did really well. Dad called me to his side and had me wash my hands and then had me sit on the stool in front of him. He placed my hands on the teats, and I began to squeeze and pull. Something was wrong. I wasn't getting any milk. Dad laughed and the old cow turned around and gave a great "moo." I think she was laughing at me also. Dad held my hands and squeezed and pulled, and I finally got those things to work. I continued on my own for a while, but I was really slow so Dad took over and finished the job. We emptied the bucket into a large milk can, and Dad started on the second cow. He was doing great, but every once in a while the old cow would swat Dad with her tail and when Dad had almost finished milking her, she swatted him across the face. Dad struck the cow on her backside, and frightened the cow jumped. The next thing I saw was her left hoof in the nearly full milk bucket. Dad cursed both in English and Slovenian.

I don't think Mom, Dad, Jake, or I were happy when Dad said he had completed the road, and we would be leaving the Muddy as we all enjoyed those few exciting weeks.

When we moved back to Crested Butte, Dad was placed on loan to supervise the Gunnison road crew and spent the rest of the summer rebuilding the road from Gunnison to Almont. The Road Commissioner of that district, Mr. Jorgenson, was very pleased with Dad's work and raised his pay by $25 a month. Including the new pay raise, Dad's monthly income was now $175. With the extra money, Dad made a trip to Montrose where he traded the old blue 1928 Chrysler that we had for many years and purchased a new 1939 black Chrysler Royal. We all liked the new black Chrysler, but we were sorry to see Dad trade in the "old shehasta."

RANCHING AND CATTLE PRODUCTION

Next to coal mining, cattle ranching was the largest industry in Crested Butte. Most of the ranches were located south of Crested Butte on the highway to Gunnison. The names of some of the ranch owners were Malensek, Kapushion, Lacy, Niccoli, Eaker, Spann, and Yaklich. The Yaklich Family is best remembered for their dairy herd and the dairy they ran in Crested Butte. These ranches were all family owned, and they very seldom did they hire help from outside their family except when the cattle were on the range and during haying season.

In late spring or early summer, depending on the last winter's snowfall, the cattlemen from south of Crested Butte would drive their cattle to the open ranges to north and west where the cattle would feed on the native grasses and plants. These grazing lands were leased from private landowners and the U. S. Forest Service. The cattle continued grazing on them until late summer or early fall and usually a cowhand or range rider, was hired to be responsible for them. The range rider was quartered in a cabin not far from his herd at the intersection of the Slate River road and the Gothic Road.

Besides overseeing the herd, the range rider was responsible for seeing that the land was not over grazed and moved his stock as necessary. He had to watch out for predators, usually coyotes and poison plants. For example, the roots of the native Larkspur (Lady Slipper) were toxic to cattle. If a cow consumed them, his stomach would bloat, and he would lie on his back with his legs in the air. The cow could be saved if found quickly enough for treatment. Once, when we were working at the Kochevar mine, we found two cows lying on their backs with their stomachs bloated and a ranch hand no where in sight. Uncle Fred and Uncle Rudy, using their pocketknives, punctured the cows somewhere in the bloated area and drained the poison. One of the two cows survived.

In late summer when the Timothy grass was matured --- haying season --- the rancher would hire help to cut, rake, and stack the hay. In most cases, it was a few high school age or somewhat younger boys from the local area. Most of them lived in a bunkhouse on the ranch, as the work was from sun up to sun down. However, the haying season lasted only a few weeks and was often interrupted by rain.

When the Timothy was mature, it was cut, mowed, and left on the ground for a few days until it dried. Once dry, it was raked and stacked with mechanical mowing machines and rakes powered by horses or mules. The raking was a two-task process. First the dry hay was raked into long rows with a horse pulling a sulky rake, which when in the down position would gather the hay. When you got to the end of the row, you would raise the rake dumping the hay. Once the hay was gathered in rows, a driver with his buck raked carried in front of a team of horses would pick up the hay and carry it to the stacking area. The buck rake and stacker were somewhat similar in design and both made from long, narrow poles. Once the hay was forked onto the stacker that was also powered by a horse it would raise the hay to the top of the stack and dump it.

I spent a few days in the haying business. I was hired to lead the stacker horse, which was the lowest paying and easiest job on the haying team. The men building a hay stack would load the long fork of the stacker with hay, and I would lead the horse forward to raise it to the top of the stack, dump the hay, and back the horse to the original starting place to be loaded again. After working on the job for two days, the rains came. Since we couldn't rake or stack wet hay, we just sat around the bunkhouse, told stories and played cards. I learned a lot about life listening to the older boys talk about their experiences. As I grew up, I also found that many of the stories they told were not true and could never happen.

We didn't get paid for the days we didn't work, but we still got charged for our bunk and meals. After a couple of days in the bunk house waiting for the rain to quit and the hay to dry, most of us hay hands walked back to Crested Butte. Once the rain quit and the hay dried, most of the boys returned to the ranch and their haying jobs but I didn't. Two days of work and a couple days of just sitting around were about a break-even deal for me. I left that job with no coins jingling in my pocket.

FUR TRADE AND OTHER FURRY TALES

TRAPPING

During the winter months, when the animal pelts were prime, several of the men in Crested Butte became fur trappers. Muskrat and ermine were the most popular prey. Ermine, also called a sloat, has a white pelt with a black tip on the end of its tail. In the warmer summer months, its fur changes from white to reddish brown, and it is then called a weasel.

Uncle Matt, who was one of these winter trappers, would work his trap line both morning and evening. I can remember him coming home with his catch and skinning both muskrat and ermine and then stretching their hides over wire frames until they dried. In the spring, a fur buyer would come to Crested Butte and set up shop for a day, buying all of the pelts that were for sale. There wasn't much haggling, as all of the trappers knew the going price at the fur market in Denver.

I did try my hand at trapping ermine with Uncle Matt. That day we walked to the cemetery, put on webs, snowshoes, and walked up the Gothic Road. We would stop at every culvert to check the traps, release and bag the ermine, (most of them were dead and frozen), reset the trap, cover it with a light coat of snow, and re-bait the entrance to the culvert. Uncle Matt would bait each culvert by tossing chicken heads, innards, and blood toward its center. Inside the culvert, at each end, he would anchor and set his trap and cover it with snow. When the ermine went to get the bait in the center of the culvert, it would step on one of the traps. Sounds simple. It was.

The year Uncle Matt went into the Navy was the same year I spent living with Grandma and Grandpa Kochevar. That year I tried my hand at trapping ermine on my own. I wasn't the diligent trapper that Uncle Matt was, and I didn't walk the trap line daily. I did catch a few ermine, but like my job at haying during the summer, I never got rich.

I never tried my hand at trapping muskrat, and I don't know the exact procedure. I do know that the traps were not baited. Muskrat are vegetarians. The traps were set and placed in the water runs that the muskrat used to get to their burrows. The burrow was a chamber on or near the water with several passages leading to it, all under water. Once the muskrat was trapped, he would drown. Muskrats stayed in their burrows during the day and moved about during the night. Most trappers tended their muskrat traps early in the morning.

MINK FARMING

In the early to mid 1940s, raising domestic mink for their pelts was a lucrative business. The four Kochevar Brothers - Uncles Fred, Rudy, Matt, and Jake - started the Kochevar Brothers' Mink Ranch in a long building they constructed near Coal Creek, behind and west of Uncle Rudy's house. The city parking lot on West Elk Avenue is now located on the land that was once Uncle Rudy's home and the Kochevar Brothers' Mink Ranch.

Since Uncle Matt and Uncle Jake were in the Navy and Uncle Rudy had a rather large family and continued to work at the Big Mine, the responsibility for housing and raising the mink fell almost entirely on Uncle Fred. Uncle Rudy and Grandpa were able, at the outset, to help Uncle Fred build the barn and multiple cages.

When the mink barn was almost completed, Uncle Fred and I made a trip to Gunnison to buy some used roofing paper to cover this nearly completed barn. New roofing material was not available, as was the case with many things, because of the war. We took off in the old Jewett pickup truck, which was built from a Jewett four door sedan. Grandpa Kochevar did the pickup conversion. He built and installed a wooden bed on the old Jewett and made a pickup cab from hand formed galvanized tin.

By the way, automobiles were manufactured under the Jewett name from 1922 through 1927.

The trip to Gunnison was trouble free, but the return to Crested Butte was a disaster. The pickup was overloaded with the heavy rolls of roofing paper and the very thin, worn tires on the pickup couldn't handle the load. We didn't get out of Gunnison before we got our first flat. The road from Gunnison to Crested Butte was gravel, and every sharp rock on the road punctured the thin overpressurized tires.

To fix a flat on the old Jewett, we had to block the wheels, jack the pickup, and remove the wheel. A special tool was used to remove the tire and the tube from the wheel. It was a screw jack mechanism that hooked to the rim of the wheel. As the screw jack was turned clockwise, it pulled in on the steel split rim, making it smaller in diameter so that you could remove the tube and the tire. This was a dangerous operation as the removal tool could, and sometimes did, release accidentally and jump off the rim with great force. Once the tube was repaired and a large rubber boot installed inside the tire, the tube and tire were remounted on the rim. The screw jack was turned counterclockwise; the rim increased to its normal diameter, and engaged the repaired tire. Change completed? Not yet! You still had to hand pump air at a high pressure into the tire and mount all on the pickup. Uncle Fred usually said a few words while hand pumping the air into the tire at a higher than normal pressure.

I don't remember how many times we had to boot the tires and patch the tubes before we got the load of roofing paper to Crested Butte. I heard Uncle Fred cuss many times before, but never like he did on this trip. He yelled out every swear word ever spoken in two languages, English and Slovenian. This trip of 28 miles took us over eight hours. I am sure we established a new record for the longest time to complete the trip from Gunnison to Crested Butte.

After the barn was finally completed and all of the cages built a large meat grinder and freezer were purchased. Hundreds of small tin cans were collected and large quantities of lettuce, tomatoes, and horsemeat had to be ground and mixed with commercial mink chow and frozen in the small cans.

Now that all of the preparations were made, it was time to finally purchase the mink. I don't remember the exact number that were purchased, but I do remember there were a pair of white, a pair of silver blue, several standard black and black variations. All of the blacks were female except for two, who were subsequently named Doc and Grandpa. The males were much larger than the females. Doc was a very aggressive businessman, and Grandpa was a gentle lover. During mating season, you soon found that some females preferred aggressive Doc and others like gentle old Grandpa.

I don't remember how often Uncle Fred had to butcher a horse or mule, but as the population of mink grew, it seemed the task came around pretty frequently. The horses were obtained from ranches in the area and mules from the Big Mine. Most were too old to work or had been injured. Getting horses or mules to butcher was not easy as there were other mink ranchers in the area competing for them and they were getting expensive.

I remember one young horse that Uncle Fred bought, named Jughead. His mother was a small riding mare and his father was a very large workhorse. Needless to say, this was not a planned marriage. Jughead had the body of his mother and the head of his father. He was kept in a corral on the west side of the Gothic road just before the cemetery bridge. The Kochevars leased this land to keep their stock until additional mink feed was needed. One day my friend Billy Lacy and I took an old saddle and bridle from the house and carried it down to the corral. We put the bridle and saddle on Jughead, and I climbed into the saddle. Jughead didn't buck, he just ran. He took off before Billy could hand me the reins. I hung on to the saddle horn as Jughead headed for the willows along Coal Creek. I should have jumped to the ground, but I didn't. I just held on. The only thing that stopped Jughead was a barbwire fence. Once he did, I jumped off and grabbed the reins. I didn't get back on him; I just led him back to the corral and removed the saddle and bridle. I looked as if I had been whipped with a quirt and drug for miles. The willows put large welts on my face and arms, and tore my shirt to shreds. I never tried to ride Jughead again.

I left Crested Butte at the end of summer, and the mink herd grew in numbers over the next few years. Just as the ranch developed into what looked like a moneymaker, mink coats lost there fashion appeal, and the price of mink pelts hit an all time low. With the high cost of feed and upkeep, it was no longer profitable to raise mink. The Kochevar brothers got out of the mink business. This venture ended up with a couple of mink coats for two of the brother's wives, mink stoles for all of the Kochevar sisters, and very little money in the Kochevar Brothers' account at the bank.

TAXIDERMY

All of the Kochevar brothers were craftsmen... a trait they inherited and learned from their father and grandfather. Give any of the boys a hammer, a saw, and other hand tools and they would design and build almost anything out of wood or metal.

I remember Uncle Jake designing lapel pins from celluloid, which was a plastic substance, used before the invention of nylon and the other synthetic plastics of today. The pins would usually depict a cartoon character. Uncle Jake would cut the celluloid with a fine saw. He would glue different colored pieces of celluloid to a white celluloid base. A drop of acetone would melt the celluloid, and the pieces would bond to each other. On the back side of the completed character, he would bond a safety pin. Uncle Jake had many scraps of celluloid, which he kept in a large cigar box. I think many of the colored pieces were from the handles of discarded tooth bushes. The pins usually depicted a cartoon character that he would trace from the comics section of the Sunday Denver Post.

Among all of this familial talent, the real artist was Uncle Matt. You could give Uncle Matt a handful of clay and a few feathers and the completed object would look as if it was about to fly away. In the early 1940s, the walls of the Kochevar house were covered with stuffed mammals, birds and insects. Grandpa Kochevar made some of the early mounts, but the ones that looked as if they could jump from the wall or fly away were the ones that were prepared and stuffed by Uncle Matt.

Uncle Matt took up taxidermy as a teenager and worked at it until he enlisted in the Navy at age 22. He mounted everything from butterflies to elk. All of the mounted animals in the Crested Butte area, that looked like they were alive, were crafted by him. His head mounts usually included a portion of the shoulder of the animal, which gave it a more lifelike appearance.

First he would process and tan the hide and order a form, which was a rough skeleton made from pressed wood pulp, paper pulp and glue, very much like papier-mâché, from a taxidermy supplier. With clay he would sculpt the lifelike features onto the form, inset glass eyes into the sculpted eye sockets and then stretch the prepared hide over the finished animal shape. Then Uncle Matt would brush its hair and hand paint features to make it look more true to life. He mounted several deer and elk heads for hunters in the Crested Butte area.

The largest game Uncle Matt ever mounted was the head of an American Buffalo that was killed at the Pueblo Zoo and then given to him. He did most of his taxidermy work in the saloon portion of the house and when the large form he had ordered, arrived, we all watched him remove it from the wooden crate and set it on the floor. Everyone passing by the house would stare at the large form. Most of the town folk kept up with the daily progress.

A few days after the form arrived, my cousin John Spritzer and I were playing in the saloon and Uncle Matt placed the form over John's head. He could actually stand up and walk in the form. The eyeholes were the size of a softball. John placed his head against the inside of the form and yelled something. I don't know what possessed me, but I doubled my fist and poked it into the eyehole, hitting cousin John smack in the eye. John cried. Uncle Matt removed the form, revealing John with his first black eye. I don't remember what my punishment was, but upon seeing the black eye, I felt very bad. I think I was about eight years old at the time, and cousin John was five. The buffalo was completed in 1940 or 1941 and was placed on the wall of the saloon. That was over 60 years ago, and it is still hanging on that wall.

FURRY FRIENDS

The Kochevar family always had live animals and pets at the house and being hunters, they invariably had dogs. Uncle Fred owned two sporting dogs, an English Setter, that as I remember was actually too old to hunt and a young English Pointer, which he named Rex. Uncle Fred worked with Rex on retrieving and all of the other skills for being a good bird-hunting dog. When pheasant season arrived, he packed Rex and some friends into this 1936 Chevy and went off to hunt in Montrose. Uncle Fred was anxious to see his well-trained pointer do his tricks in the field. Rex worked in front of the hunters and soon stopped and pointed at some bushes. A large cock pheasant flew from the bushes, the hunters shot and the pheasant fell, and Rex, he ran as fast as he could back toward the car. His hunting was over. When the hunters arrived back at the car, after the hunt, the prize hunting dog was still shaking. Uncle Fred had trained him well except he had never fired a gun near Rex prior to the hunt. Afterwards, Uncle Fred took a real ribbing from everyone in town, as his buddies couldn't wait to tell the story about Fred's prize hunting dog, Rex. I don't think Uncle Fred ever took old Rex hunting again.

The Kochevar's also had several cats that they fed in the woodshed and the shop area. There was nothing spectacular about the cats. They weren't friendly. They were just survivors and kept the mice population to a minimum.

Then there was Maggie. She was a magpie that Uncle Matt brought home when she was very young. He built a large cage for her, and placed it near the front window of the saloon, which was also near to where he worked on his taxidermy. Maggie was never lonely as someone was talking to her all the time therefore she developed quite a vocabulary. She knew her name and would say hello to everyone. Maggie was also an alarm clock. Grandma would let her out of her cage, and she would fly to the boys' bedroom and screech, "Matt, Jake, time to get up; time for school." She would continue to screech these words until the boys got up. She would also screech, "Matt, Jake, get up; time to go to church." I don't remember if she only used that chant on Sundays. But like I said, she was a pretty smart bird.

OTHER JOBS AND BUSINESSES

POLL TAX

Every man in Crested Butte over the age of 21 was assessed a poll tax of two dollars a year. You could pay the two dollars or you could spend a day working for the city, which set two days aside each year, usually right before Memorial Day, when the men could work for their poll tax. This was the annual city cleanup. Rather than spend eight hours cleaning up Crested Butte, many of the men would rather pay the two dollars. Kids could work in place of their fathers, uncles, or friends and would be paid the two dollars by the person for whom they were working. I don't think there was an age limit for working at these jobs. I worked the poll tax for my Dad and Uncle Fred when I was 10 years old.

On the scheduled days, all of the workers, mostly kids, met in front of the jailhouse, with rake in hand, ready for work. The first day we cleaned all of the streets and alleys in town. The second day we raked the road to the cemetery. The younger kids did the raking, and the older boys and men shoveled the trash into trucks and hauled the trash to the city dump. Four dollars for a weekend of work was big money for any youngster in the early 1940s.

LOCAL BUSINESSES

The labor market in Crested Butte would not be complete without mentioning the local businesses.

The Crested Butte Light and Water Company, located just across Coal Creek to the west of the City Hall, provided electricity and water to homes in Crested Butte. Electrical power was used primarily for lights but not all of the homes in Crested Butte were wired for electricity. A large water-powered wheel, supplemented by a coal-fired steam boiler generated the electrical power. As kids, we watched the two large pipes exhaust hot steam and water into Coal Creek. At the entrance to the building was an office where you paid you electric and water bill and the warm steam boiler inside the building seemed to also generate friends, as many of the locals sat around the boiler and talked and played cards.

As mentioned in a previous chapter, the C.F.&I. controlled a large portion of the businesses in Crested Butte. They owned the large Company Store, a service station, and the hotel. Uncle J.N. Schaefer managed and ran the hotel for the C.F.&I.

A hardware store, which was locally owned, sold everything. You could buy gas and fuel there as well as purchase hunting and fishing licenses. Like the Electric Company, it had a large pot belly stove and a few chairs that were never empty.

There were two and sometimes three General Merchandise / Grocery Stores. There were also five saloons and two liquor stores. I think the saloons got more business than the grocery stores.

The busiest place in town around 1:00 p.m. every weekday was the Post Office. The mail truck came in from Gunnison shortly after noon, and then the mail clerks would begin sorting and posting the mail. When finished, the clerks would open the window for business. Almost everyone had a postal box with a combination lock on it. The door of each postal box had a window in it so you could tell at a glance if you had mail. If you didn't have a postal box, you waited in line at one of the windows to check with the clerk whether or not you had any mail to pick up.

There was also a drugstore in town, which was a hangout for most of the older kids. I guess you would call it "the teenage hangout." Groups of teens would meet there before movies and games and plan their evenings. The drug store had the only pay telephone in Crested Butte. With only a few telephones in the town, it did a pretty good business and many of the folks in town used it to keep in touch with family and friends. The telephone was also busy with the teenagers using it to call friends who had a home telephone.

The price for a local call was a nickel, but many of the boys found a way of beating that price. They would put a penny in the nickel slot, hold it in the slot with minimal pressure and place a table knife blade over the top edge of the penny. Sharply forcing the penny down the slot with the knife blade would activate the phone. Some of the boys made fake nickels (slugs) out of metal to use in the telephone. I don't think the telephone was a paying proposition when the boys were using it.

The telephones in Crested Butte were all manual and when you lifted the receiver and put your nickel in it, if it was a pay phone, you heard the voice of the local telephone operator saying, "Operator, How can I help you?" Once she knew the party to whom you wished to speak she would manually switch you to that person. The local operator was Esther Gibson. She had the telephone switchboard in a front room of her house. Being a pre-teen, I found that I was not among the "in crowd" and only went to the drugstore for ice cream or a fountain drink.

Uncle Rudy Kochevar ran the part time barbershop in Crested Butte, during evenings when he came home from the coal mine and on Saturdays. Uncle Rudy never smoked, but he loved his chew, Copenhagen, and always had a wad of it under his lip while cutting hair. He had a spittoon near the barber chair and never missed less than ten feet away. When the mine closed in 1952, Uncle Rudy became a full time barber in Pueblo. The hardest part of his transition to city life was giving up his chew. He would stick a bit of chew under his lip but when a customer arrived for a hair cut, he would have to either run to the back room to spit it out or just swallow it. After several months of swallowing the Copenhagen, he was finally able to kick the habit.

Most of the population in Crested Butte was able to get by dealing with the local businesses but a trip to Gunnison always gave you a better selection, and often lower prices. However, less than one fourth of the families in Crested Butte owned an automobile and the 28 miles of washboard road was not a pleasurable trip. You always knew who made the trip to Gunnison during the week, as it was always mentioned in the local weekly newspaper.

Clothing and many other items, including some livestock, could be purchased from the mail-order houses. Everyone had catalogs from Montgomery Ward, Sears & Roebuck, Spiegel, and the Chicago Mail Order House. When the year ended, and new catalogs arrived, the old page-worn catalogs took their place on a shelf in the outhouse.

CHAPTER 4: ENTERTAINMENT

MOVIE THEATER

Wow! No television and only about one radio for every ten families! What did we do?

We had a movie theater that played two different movies each week. One movie was shown midweek, and the other was on the weekend, plus there was a matinee every Sunday and Holiday.

At about thirty minutes before show time we would line up in front of the theater. Some of us had money, and the others were willing to work to see the featured movie, cartoon, newsreel and the serial. The serial always ended with a damsel in distress or some other danger about to unfold. We could hardly wait until the following week to see if the heroine would be rescued. The kids who selected to work for their ticket were usually the same ones every week. I think the theater owner knew which kids didn't have money to pay to see the movie. Those workers swept the theater after the movie or changed the marquee, which was black tin letters placed against an opaque glass background. With the lights turned on in the evening we could read the title of the movie playing and the days of the week it would play. If we wanted more detail, we could walk to the theater and read the movie poster that was placed in a locked glass covered frame, where we could get the movie details a week in advance of the showing. Most of the movies were black and white, but Technicolor made its debut in the late 1930s and early 1940s. I remember seeing "The Wizard of Oz" and "Gone With the Wind" at the theater in Crested Butte.

MUSIC

When walking the main street of Crested Butte, as a youngster, I could always hear music, usually accordion music coming from at least one of the many saloons in town.

Dad's Buddies
TOP: Rudy Saya, Matt Slogar, Dad, Fred Kochevar, Paul Sterk.
BOTTOM: Paul Panion, Emit Caboi

Uncle John Spritzer not only knew every musical group in town but he, himself, was an integral part of the scene. The following is related from my many conversations and recordings with Uncle John.

Uncle John recounted that Crested Butte at one time had a marching band with almost 20 members that performed for many occasions, but was most famous for playing at and leading the annual Fourth of July parade. The bandleader was Ephraim Bailey who also played a large bass tuba in the band.

I asked Uncle John about some of the local bands that I had heard about and he was quick to inform me that they were not bands but orchestras. Some of these orchestras of the 1920s and 1930s and the members that John could remember were:

- The Bill Bailey Orchestra. Bill played the clarinet, Peggy Arnott was at the piano, Joe Velotti on drums, and Hank Arnot played the saxophone.
- The Merrimakers. Joe Saya was the leader and played the saxophone. Charlie Pasic played the trumpet, Lawrence Perko the saxophone and one of the Caricatos played the drums.
- The Spritzer Ochestra. Mr. Spritzer, (Uncle John's Dad) was the leader and played the tamburitza, which is a string instrument similar to a mandolin in shape and sound. It is the most common of the national instruments of Croatia. Martin (Uncle John's brother) played the fiddle, Mike Fisher the bass fiddle, and Uncle John Spritzer, at the age of 15, played the accordion.

The Spritzer Orchestra played every Saturday night for a dance held at the Croation Hall. When he first started playing with the band, John said, after playing for several hours, his arms and back ached and he was very glad to hear his Dad announce a slow dance as the last dance for the evening.

Other than the Croation Hall, dances were held upstairs over the Gus Mattivi Saloon. This building was later known as Frank and Gal's Bar and is now the Eldo. There were also dances held at the Glacier SchoolHouse.

During the 40s, many of the local musicians were in the military service, and orchestras broke up. The remaining musicians joined forces and formed an orchestra that would play on special occasions.

Some musicians also played solo like John Spritzer, Botsa Spritzer, Joe Starika, and Emil Lunk. They all played the accordion except for Emil Lunk who played a concertina-like instrument called a bandonium.

Uncle John Spritzer learned to play the accordion from his brother Tony who learned from Uncle Joe Starika. Uncle John remembered, as a young boy, going to the Starika's to listen to the accordion music. The Starikas lived near the Big Mine tipple and ran a boarding house and accordion music could be heard coming from it every weekend. Some of the local girls would go to the Starika house to dance with the boarders and Mrs. Starika would sell homebrew for 25 cents a glass.

LODGES AND CLUBS

I think almost everyone in town belonged to a lodge, which played an important part of your social life in Crested Butte. There was a need to belong to something other than "The Company." The lodges not only filled that need but they also provided you with a life insurance policy. Monthly dues were collected and meetings, dances, and parties were held. When a lodge member died, that member's beneficiary would collect a sum of money, usually $1000, which was a large amount at that time.

In the early 1900s there were Mason Lodges, Croatian Lodges, and Slovenian Lodges. Being Slovenian, our family belonged to one of the Slovenian Lodges, and therefore it's the only one with which I'm familiar. This Lodge was called S.N.P.J. or *Slovenska Narodna Podporna Jednota,* (Slovenian National Benefit Society). The Chapter was the *Planinski Orel,* (Plains Eagle). Dad was a paid member of the Lodge, and I was a Junior Member.

The S.N.P.J. was a very active lodge and sponsored several dances and parties each year. During Memorial Day all the members and children in town would march behind the military to the cemetery and return to the Croatian Hall for a party. The elders would dance and drink, and the children were given candy and soda pop.

When a lodge member died, the living lodge members would march behind the hearse to

S.N.P.J. Lodge Badge.

the cemetery, dressed in their best coat and pants, a white shirt, tie and their Plains Eagle Lodge badge. A handshake was depicted on the badge and below it there was reversible ribbon that was red, white, and blue with gold lettering on one side and black with silver lettering on the reverse side, that showed the lodge name, number and chapter. For a funeral you wore the black side of the ribbon outward and afterwards, you reversed the ribbon and wore the patriotic red, white, blue.

Many of the women in Crested Butte had their own social clubs. Mom, all of my aunts, and several friends formed a group called the Busy Bees, which was a women's sewing circle, at least that's what its charter said. The women would meet at a different member's home every week, I think on Tuesday night. The hostess for the week would be responsible for serving coffee and refreshments. The women would sit in the living room and sew, knit, embroider or crochet sharing stories and telling jokes the entire time. Cousin Jouette and I were about five years old, so our mothers would take us to the meetings. We knew when the ladies were telling jokes because they would spell out many of the words and always the punch line. When Jouette and I started school and learned to spell, we were no longer taken to the Busy Bee meetings. I was always amazed at how the ladies could talk and laugh and never lose a stitch.

HAPPY HOUR

The most widely attended form of entertainment in Crested Butte was "happy hour" at one of the local pool halls or taverns. Most of the men had "happy hour" after dinner as dinner was usually eaten as soon as the men got home from the mines. However, there were always some of the townsfolk who stopped in for a "fast one" after work and were still there after dinner. There were also a few men who were there when the bars opened and stayed until closing time. No bar in Crested Butte was ever forced to close for lack of business.

CHAPTER 5: FISHING

    Fishing in Crested Butte has never been better than it was fifty years ago. The fish were much more plentiful, and from what I have read, much healthier than they are today. The reason for this degradation is not over-fishing. Fifty years ago more locals and tourists fished the streams than they do today. The catch limit was twenty fish at least 7 inches long, for each licensed fisherman and ten fish for children under 16 years of age with no license. Today the limit is so small that you can't catch enough fish in a day for a single meal.

    If the problem isn't over-fishing, my guess is that it's from pollution of our lakes and streams. I've read just recently about the closing of a large guest lodge because of a leaking sewage system. Articles have also recently been written about the quality of the sewage drainage systems from other areas around Crested Butte.

    When I was growing up in the early 1940's, I went fishing several times a week. Fishing was not only a sport but also a supplement to the dinner table. I, with fly rod in hand, could start fishing in Coal Creek behind the powerhouse on Second and Elk Avenues, fish the creek to the bridge on First Street and have my limit of ten fish all over seven inches long. Today there are no fish in Coal Creek down stream of the ore mine runoff about two miles west of town.

We were polluters of the creek 50 years ago also. Everyone who lived along Coal Creek dumped their outdoor privies and garbage into it, but this pollution never seemed to kill the fish. The fishing gear used today is much superior to what we had when I fished in the area back then. For example, no one had spinning or casting gear. Your progressed from a willow, string and hook to a bamboo or steel fly rod, which was used for bait fishing, as well as fly fishing. The fly reel, manual or automatic was also used for bait fishing. A fishing buddy of mine went bait fishing with me one day with his fly rod and an open face casting reel. Every time he cast his line, he spent 10 minutes untangling it from the backlash. He spent more time cussing and untangling that he did fishing. He used his fly reel the next time we went out fishing. Fishing rivers and streams was not a big problem with fly gear, but it was difficult to get your bait into the deep water on many of the lakes.

I think the biggest advancement in fishing was the nylon fishing line (monophyoment). Prior to the mid-1940's, we used only silk or rayon, waxed and braided fly lines with "cat gut" leaders, which were very hard and brittle when they were dry and broke if bent sharply. Once you removed your leader from your fly book, you had to soak it in water until it became pliable. Only then could you tie it to your fly line. This was also true with your handmade artificial flies, as the short leader on your flies was also made from gut.

Early summer, after the high spring runoff depleted somewhat, every fisherman dusted off his fishing gear and with spade in hand, went to the garden to dig worms. Everyone bait fished until mid to late summer when the water turned clear and trout would rise to a fly. Most of the bait fishing was done with local angleworms or store bought salmon eggs. Some fishermen had good luck using small metallic spinners and working them while fishing in the deep holes along the banks of the rivers.

Later in the summer, when the waters turned clear, fishermen traded their worms for artificial flies that came in many colors and sizes. However, most of the fishermen used only six or eight basic flies on a six-foot long, three fly gut leader. Most fishermen, like the hunters of the area, would not tell you where the best fishing was or what flies were attracting the fish. The best place to get this information was the local hardware store or fly supplier, who could at least tell you which fly was selling the best. I always went to my Aunt Rose Starika. She tied flies as a hobby and sold them to many of the fishermen in Crested Butte.

LEFT: The writer at Coal Creek, 1937. RIGHT: The writer and Uncle Jake on Slate River with fish caught by Uncle Fred on Taylor River. BELOW: Late 1920's, suckers from Peanut Lake.

If you were like most fishermen, and used a three-fly leader, you would tie a multi-colored fly to the lead fly position. Those flies were mostly Royal Coachman or Rio Grande King. The second fly was usually one of the Gray Hackles with a colored body, usually yellow, orange, red or peacock. The third fly could be a Black Gnat, Pink Lady, or a Woolly Worm. You exchanged these flies as you fished until you got the combination that best attracted the trout.

There is nothing more gratifying or exciting than making a beautiful cast of the three flies into the ripples under a large rock in the middle of the stream, seeing a silver flash in the water and feeling a jerk on the fly rod. Your immediate reaction is to set the hook, and bamboo rod bends to its extreme and then work your trophy to the shore. It's a beautiful flopping 10-inch native trout. One never forgets this experience!

That same exhilarating experience was available to everyone in Crested Butte 50 years ago, and as children we took full advantage of it. We fished Coal Creek from the cemetery bridge to just short of Kebler Pass, Slate River from the white schoolhouse to Pittsburgh, and East River behind Crested Butte Mountain. We fished every stream or river we could get to on foot. A fishing trip to the East River was the most difficult but also the most rewarding. We would start off from Crested Butte and go north on the gothic Road just short of Snodgrass Mountain. Then we walked down a steep trail behind Crested Butte Mountain to East River. The trail from the Gothic Road to East River, called Indian Trail, wasn't too difficult in getting to the river but the walk back up the steep trail in wet clothes, fly rod in hand, and 10 large trout strung on a willow branch in the other was a challenging feat of courage. Once you got back to the Gothic Road it was down hill to Crested Butte.

As kids, we fished Coal Creek more than any other stream. The fish were generally smaller, but plentiful, and we just had to step out of our back yard with fly rod, reel, some flies, and a pocketknife and start fishing. No one carried a creel. When we caught our first trout we cut a large willow with a "V" yoke and strung the fish on it. To keep the fish from drying out and shrinking, we usually dropped the willow with the fish on it in shallow water while we were casting for more. Everyone marked his or her fly rods with a line carved around the cork grip exactly seven inches from the butt of the rod. We always measured the fish in question and sometimes we even stretched them a little to make the mark. We kept the fish wet as we couldn't afford any shrinking.

The best stream fishing was Taylor River from Almont to the dam. The river was deep and fast running and not a place for children or the inexperienced fisherman. Chest-high waders and a net on a straight long pole were necessary equipment as the swift current was nearly waist high. You used the net to support yourself as you worked the river. You never had to bother measuring the fish you caught on the Taylor, as it usually only took only a few to fill your creel. If you caught your limit you would have to empty your creel more than once. One year we had a family fish fry at the Taylor Campgrounds. The men went fishing early in the day and fished for several hours. Dinner consisted of this fresh caught trout with all the trimmings. I have never seen so many large trout as I did that day.

It was always the fisherman's responsibility to clean his own trout. So we were taught this procedure at an early age and usually always cleaned the fish in the stream before we brought them home.

Uncle Martin (Teenie) Tezak told me the following story about one of his fishing experiences on Slate River. He was bait fishing in Slate River north of Peanut Lake. He tossed the worm bait into a deep hole near the bank and it drifted on the bottom of the river only a short way when there was a thrashing in the water and his pole bent double. He had hooked a real whopper. He tried to land the fish but he couldn't get it up the bank. Managing to wrap his fishing line around a large spruce tree nearby he was able to tie off the line, and ran back to Crested Butte to get help. He and one of the Volk boys returned to the scene of the big catch. When they arrived they found that the fish, the line and the tree were all gone. All that was left was a large hole where the tree was torn from it roots.

The largest trout I ever caught was north of Gothic when several members of the Kochevar family went on a picnic at the Gothic Campgrounds. The men left the campgrounds early in the morning and hiked to an ore mine they were prospecting on one of the mountains north west of Rustlers' Gulch. The women gabbed away while they prepared the meal for the men on their return and the children helped and then played on the banks of the river. My two cousins, Johnnie and Rudy and I went fishing. I walked to the bridge crossing the river and fished the river back to the campgrounds. After over an hour I had caught only a few keepers. Once more, I tossed my flies toward a narrow deep hole in the river and just as the lead fly hit the water, the fish struck the fly. I was startled. I knew that I had never caught anything this large before. It was not the classical, working the fish scene you see on television. Once I had him hooked I ran down the stream dragging the fish to a rocky beach. Once on the beach, I jumped on the flopping fish and grabbed him with both hands. I took him further away from the water before I dislodged the hook. He was a great fish; a rainbow trout, and I couldn't wait to show him off. I went back to the campgrounds with trout in hand to show everyone. I could hardly wait for Dad to return from his prospecting trip. The rainbow weighed over three pounds.

Cousins

John Tezak, Joe Tezak, the writer, Leonard Tezak, Jouette Bruno

I also fished most of the lakes around Crested Butte, but always seemed to return to Erwin Lake and Emerald Lake. Lake fishing was usually bait fishing. The fish would rise to a fly in the early evening but we always had better luck the rest of the time using worms or salmon eggs. As I mentioned earlier, we only had fly rods and reels and casting was limited, but if you were patient and persistent you could catch your limit most of the time. Dad loved lake fishing more that stream fishing as he enjoyed the solitude while sitting on a rock, sipping a beer, waiting for the pole tip to move so that he could set the hook.

One evening in early summer, Uncle Joe Starika came over to Gramdma Kochevar's house. It was the same summer that I was living with Grandma. He asked me if I wanted to go fishing with him the next morning and I became very excited when Grandma nodded that I could go. I didn't ask any questions because I knew Uncle Joe would tell me everything he wanted me to know. He said I was to dress warmly, and dress to walk some distance in the snow and that he could pick me up at eight o'clock the next morning, with all of the fishing gear needed for the trip. At eight o'clock sharp the next morning his 1934 tan Ford Coupe stopped in front of Grandma's. I grabbed my coat, hat, and gloves and we were off. I had no idea where we were going but we soon headed west toward Kebler Pass. Uncle Joe finally said that we were going fishing at Erwin Lake. We drove west until we got to the Erwin cutoff and parked the car as the road to Erwin was still covered with several feet of snow. Uncle Joe unloaded the fishing gear, handed me my share and we started walking to the lake. There was a heavy crust on the snow, making it easier to walk and preventing us from sinking. We stopped on the southwest side of the lake, a spot I had never fished before but Uncle Joe knew exactly where he was going. The water near the shoreline was covered with a thin layer of ice. Uncle Joe broke through it near to the shore where we were standing and reached into his creel, retrieving a can opener and a can. The can said "Tender Garden Peas." Uncle Joe opened it and tossed a handful of the peas into the lake where he had broken the ice. We proceeded to rig our poles and put a couple of peas on the hook for bait. It wasn't long before I got a nibble and the first strike. I reeled in an eight-inch trout. Uncle Joe laughed. He then dug a large hole in the snow and told me to toss the fish into it to keep it fresh and cold. After a couple of hours of fishing, Uncle Joe said it was time to go. The large hole in the snow was full of fish and we had a long walk back to the car. Uncle Joe tossed the remaining peas into the lake, filled his creel, and an additional sugar sack with the fish. The walk back to the car was not easy as the sun had melted the crust and we sank into the snow with every step.

This trip reminded me of a story I heard years ago about polar bear hunting in Alaska. "The best way to catch a polar bear was to dig a large hole in the ice and line the ice around the hole with tender garden peas. When the polar bear came out of the water hole to take a pea you would kick him in the ice hole."

CHAPTER 6:
HUNTING

    Pick up any newspaper today and you can read about a crime committed by an individual using a firearm or maybe a shooting in a schoolyard by a young student.
    When I was growing up in Crested Butte in the 1930s and 1940s, guns were a part of every boy's life. Most of us, if our parents could afford one, owned a Daisy Red Ryder B.B. Gun by the time we were eight or nine years old. They were always the number one item in your letter to Santa. I remember when I got my first Red Ryder. I was eight years old, almost nine. It was under the tree when I awoke Christmas morning. I knew it would be there, but I was still very excited when I opened the box and removed my shiny new Red Ryder BB Gun. After holding the gun and admiring it for a short time, Dad had me put it back into the box. He said that I could take it outside after breakfast and should open the rest of my presents. I did, but for the life of me, I couldn't remember what any of them was.
    After a hurried breakfast I waited for Dad to say the magic words. When he had finished eating he told me I could take the BB Gun out of the box. We put on our jackets and hats and went outside onto the front porch, gun in hand. The sun was shining and my eyes squinted from the glare of the bright snow. Dad set up a target on the back shed near the creek. He reached into his pocket and handed me a cylindrical shaped red box of copper-coated BB pellets. He

mentioned a few rules like, no loaded guns in the house and where and where not to point the gun. Under Dad's supervision I was allowed to load the gun. I knew all about loading, cocking and firing the Red Ryder as many of my friends already had guns. Still, under Dad's watchful eye, I was able to cock the BB Gun and fire at the target. I did a great job of playing the new student. With a few cautions and again rules on proper gun handling, I was left on my own with my new Red Ryder.

By summer, when the grass was green and the chipmunks were running in the wild, BBs became scarce. The copper-coated little balls were no longer available, as the copper was needed for the war effort. I handled my copper BBs as if they were gold. Uncle Fred came to my rescue. He cut open a shotgun shell (I don't remember the shot size) and gave me the lead shot to use as BBs. The lead shot would only make a small dent in a tin can and wouldn't break a bottle like the copper-coated BBs would. But biggest problem was that lead shot was not all the same size and just as you had a target in your sights and squeezed the trigger, the shot would lodge in the gunbarrel. A short, stiff, wire rod was used to dislodge the lead BB and became a mandatory part of your hunting gear.

On the whole, however, we were more dependent on our side arm. It could always be seen hanging from our right hip pocket --- a beanie/sling shot. The beanies were made from a strong Y-shaped willow limb with rubber straps from a prewar, natural rubber tire inner tube, and a pocket made of soft leather from the tongue of an old workshoe. With a lot of practice and our pants' pocket full of small smooth stones, our accuracy became pretty good. Not as good as the BB gun, but we had a lot more fire power and ammunition was cheaper and always available.

At about this same time we were introduced to the 22 Rifle. Usually a parent, relative or friend would take us out to plink at the cans or other targets. Again, not only safety rules were stressed, but also the killing power of the 22.

While living with Grandma Kochevar in 1942 and 1943, I had an old, rolling block, single shot 22 rifle available to me and would go out plinking whenever I could afford a box of 22 shorts. I was told that it was necessary to clean the rifle after each use and was taught how to clean it. With special permission, I could also use Uncle Fred's Remington 22 semi-automatic rifle. It would only fire semi automatically using 22 long rifle bullets that cost twice as much as the 22 shorts.

One morning I went plinking with a couple of friends, the Gibson boys, John and Jimmy. I had the 22 semi-automatic and John had a 22 rifle. Jimmy carried his BB Gun. Walking on our way to Smith Hill, we stopped to shoot at a few cans at the city dump and then proceeded on our way. It was a great day and when we got to Nickelson Lake, we decided to walk to the Kochevar Mine on the hill north of the lake.

About 100 yards before we got to the mine tipple, we jumped two deer in an Aspen grove. The two doe ran toward the mine tipple and as we were stalking them we saw them again under the tipple. Again, the deer jumped and started to run. I put my sights on the lead doe and pulled the trigger. She fell. When we got to her, she was dead. We didn't know what to do. We looked around to see if anyone had seen us but there was no one within miles. We dragged the deer back to the Aspen grove, hung it in a tree, head down, and proceeded to clean her. I knew the Gibson boys had never cleaned a deer before but I had cleaned many rabbits. When this task was done, we began our long walk back to Crested Butte and discussed what we should do.

This was mid-summer and deer-hunting season is always in the late fall. Should we leave the deer to waste and tell no one, or should we tell someone and suffer the consequences? John and Jimmy said that they were afraid to tell their parents and left it up to me. Since I was living with Grandma and Uncle Fred I knew that I had to tell him. I was not looking forward to Uncle Fred coming home from the Big Mine. In fact, I postponed the conversation as long as I could.

After dinner Uncle Fred sat on the couch, took out his cigarette holder, placed a Camel in the holder and lit the cigarette. He always smoked a cigarette after dinner before going out for the evening. This would be my last opportunity. I sat next to him and told him I had borrowed his 22 Rifle and killed a deer. I told him it was cleaned and where we had left it. I don't remember what Uncle Fred said, but he wasn't angry.

Late that night, Uncle Fred and one of his friends drove his 1936 Chevy into the garage, (the old Blacksmith shop), unloaded the deer and skinned and quartered it. Skinning and quartering a deer late at night in the old blacksmith shop was not new to Uncle Fred. He provided the family and his friends with fresh meat all year long. Next to his 30.06 Rifle, his spotlight was his most useful hunting tool.

Big game hunting has undergone major changes in the last 50 years. Game is more plentiful today. Today we hunt for trophies. Fifty years ago we hunted for meat. Technology has provided better and more accurate firearms and we now have vehicles that can go anywhere. Even the clothing we wear is lighter, warmer, and safer. No one had heard of blaze-orange 50 years ago. Red was thought to be the most visible color so hunters usually wore a red bandanna pinned or sewn to their hats and on the back of their hunting coats.

Opening day of hunting season was a contest to see who could kill the first buck and bring it into town. The first dead buck was draped over the front fender of an automobile and parked in front of one of the several saloons on Elk Avenue before noon on opening day. It was usually draped over the right front fender of a tan 1934 Ford Coupe. This coupe was owned by Uncle Joe (Sharkey) Starika.

Every hunter had his favorite place or places to hunt. The hunting areas depended on the weather. If there was snow on the ground, the game would migrate to the lower ground. If warm and dry, they would stay in the high mountains. To every hunter, his area was a guarded secret and he wouldn't tell anyone where he was going to hunt or when he made his kill.

In 1942 when I was just nine years old I went on my first deer hunt. Wearing my warm clothes decorated in red bandannas, I drove with Uncle Jake Kochevar toward Gunnison stopping just north of Almont. There were several inches of snow on the ground and we knew the deer would be down low in the valley. It was still dark when we walked into a large grove of Aspen trees. We sat and waited. At sunup we could see several large openings from our position in the trees. We weren't waiting long when we heard the first shots but looked around and saw nothing moving.

Within minutes we heard a second group of shots and saw a doe and a fawn run by only to stop within a few feet of us and then and bound off. In the distance, I spotted another deer. It was cautious and stayed in the trees. I grabbed Uncle Jake and pointed the deer out to him. We watched as it got closer. It was a buck! Something startled him and he started to run. Uncle Jake shouldered the rifle, aimed and squeezed the trigger.

The buck continued to run only a short distance and fell. We ran in the snow toward the deer and noticed that he was not dead, but wounded. Uncle Jake decided to approach the buck grab him by the horns and cut his throat but he never completed the task. The buck swung his head violently and tossed Uncle Jake, head over heels, into the snow.

Startled and surprised, Uncle Jake brushed some of the snow from his face and clothes, took the rifle that I was now holding and shot the buck a second time killing it. Uncle Jake had finished the task he had earlier attempted. He cleaned the deer and we spent rest of the morning dragging it to the car.

Ordinarily elk hunting was not a one-day event. Preparations for elk hunting were made days in advance of the hunt, and the hunt usually lasted several more.

My first elk hunt was the following year after my first deer hunt with Uncle Jake. I was now ten years old. The members of the hunting party were Pete Marasco, Rudolph (Ruda) Sporcich, Uncle Rudy Kochevar, Uncle Fred Kochevar, my Dad and me.

Preparations were made and two days before the elk season started, we departed from Crested Butte for a cabin in a high valley in Spring Creek. I think the cabin was located in Deadman's Gulch. Since everyone worked during that day it was late afternoon by the time we left Crested Butte. Some of the hunter's were in an old Ford dump truck filled with supplies for several days and others in Dad's 1939 Chrysler Royal (no four-wheel drive or off-road vehicles). Just at dark, Uncle Rudy got the Ford dump truck stuck in the mud trying to get around a beaver dam.

We worked well into dark draining the beaver dam and building a road of rock so that we could continue. Late that night we arrived at the cabin tired, wet, cold and hungry. With a Coleman lantern as our only light, we unloaded the supplies and made a fire in the little wood stove. Ruda had sliced hard salami and bread for dinner. He also passed around a bottle of whiskey and everyone had one or two large snorts. I had a sip. Our clothes were hung to dry and we all fell asleep. I don't remember the accommodations, but there were two beds. The cabin had been closed for years.

The next morning I awoke early only to find everyone else was already dressed and moving about. Ruda was busy frying bacon and eggs and the coffee was perking. Everything smelled so good. I looked around the cabin and noticed that in the light it looked different. I mentioned that the cabin had been closed for several years; well, it wasn't closed to rodents. The place was covered with shredded cardboard from its walls, cotton from the mattresses, and rodent droppings.

After breakfast the men took to the mountains looking for game trails so they could prepare the plans for the next day's hunt. I stayed with Ruda and we spent most of the morning cleaning the cabin and putting the food and gear away.

Before he left Dad told me that if I had a chance to get away, I might want to shoot a young deer for camp meat. So after we got the cabin in good order, Ruda handed me his 30-30 lever action rifle and I started up the mountain. I found a place in the upper valley where I could see several clearings and still keep the cabin in sight. I sat in the warm sun, using a large rock as a backrest. With my binoculars I scanned every foot of the valley but I didn't see any game. Being by myself on the mountain with a rifle, I felt like Davey Crockett or maybe one of the outdoorsmen from a Zane Grey novel.

It was very comfortable in the warm sun and the "great white hunter" nodded off. I didn't sleep long. When I awoke, I looked all around to see if anyone had caught me sleeping. But who would be watching me? I was all alone up there. I resumed scouting the area with the binoculars and then got up and stretched---still no game. It wasn't long until I saw the men returning back to the cabin from their scouting mission. It was time for me to wander down the mountain back to the cabin. No camp meat!

When I got to the cabin, one of the men asked, "Where is the deer, or do we have to eat cold salami again?" I told them I hadn't seen anything and they kidded me a bit but let it go. Ruda had food cooking on the old woodstove. It wasn't salami but food he had purchased for the trip to take care of emergencies like this.

I joined the men and listened to their conversations and strategy for the morning hunt. They had spotted fresh game signs but saw no game. They decided that Dad and I would go to a selected spot and watch for game. Uncle Fred would go to another selected spot and do the same. Uncle Rudy and Pete would hike through the woods toward our spots in an attempt to scare the game toward us. Since Dad and Uncle Fred would have the best chance of making a kill, they were to use the best guns. Uncle Fred had his Remington 30.06 and Dad borrowed Uncle Rudy's 300 Savage.

The next morning, very early, Ruda had breakfast ready. After we ate, Ruda fixed a scrambled egg sandwich, wrapped it in butcher paper and stuffed it in my knapsack. I looked around. No one else was taking any food with them. Ruda said, "You'll be hungry before you get back to camp." Dad looked at me, smiled, and agreed that it could be a long time before we made it back. Ruda handed me the 30.30 and a box of shells. He wasn't going on the hunt.

It was still dark when Dad, Uncle Fred, and I left the cabin. We circled the mountain and proceeded to our selected spots. After we had traveled about an hour, Uncle Fred wished us luck and took another trail to his spot.

We finally arrived at an area above the valley and Dad said, "This is it." I couldn't see much as it was still dark. We removed our knapsacks and settled down to wait for the sunlight and the elk. Getting comfortable was difficult, as it was very cold. I wished that I had the large warm rock I fell asleep against the previous afternoon. When it was light enough to see, Dad pointed out the trails where we might see elk movement. He then walked off into the woods behind us and when he returned, I remember him saying, "There's nothing colder than a belly full of hot pee."

After waiting a long time we heard rustling sounds in the trees to our right. Dad tapped me on the shoulder, pressed his finger to his lips, and pointed to the trail in that same direction. A large cow elk had just appeared. She stopped to look into the clearing. Dad raised the 300 Savage and fired. The elk turned and ran down the trail. Dad fired a second time. We couldn't see the elk anymore, as the trail was steep and wooded.

Dad said, "Damn, I missed it." As we ran down the trail we found fresh blood and broken Aspen. About 100 yards down the hill we found the large elk. It was dead. Dad hadn't missed. In fact, he had placed both bullets within inches of the elk's heart. Dad bled the elk and removed its intestines, saving both the liver and the heart. He put them in a clean white flour sack and I carried them up the hill where we had left the knapsack. Then he fired three quick shots into the air, which signaled for help. We waited for some time before the other hunters arrived at our spot.

Ruda was right; during this wait I got hungry and ate the egg sandwich. It was the best egg sandwich I had ever eaten. I then put the still warm liver and heart in my knapsack.

After everyone had admired the large elk and congratulated Dad, the work began. Since there was no way we could carry or drag the elk back up the steep hill and then down the trail to the cabin, someone had suggested that we construct an Indian type travois. Aspen were cut into poles that were lashed with rope and belts forming four crude travois. The elk was quartered with its hide left on for protection and the Indian- fashion drag began. Going up the hill it took two men to manage each travois but one man could drag the travois with the elk going downhill.

It took most of the afternoon with many stops and profanities in at least three different languages before we could see the cabin in the distance. I was tired and the knapsack cut into my shoulders. I also carried the weight of the two rifles that had been slung over them. Once we saw the cabin, everyone seemed to gain energy and our tired bodies moved a little faster. I ran ahead to tell Ruda about our exciting day. Fresh liver, and heart fried with onions was the entree for dinner that night.

The following morning was a repeat of the hunting pattern of the previous day except the positions and the guns were changed. We were still tired from the day before when we started the hunt. Today, Uncle Fred, Dad and I would be on the chase and Uncle Rudy, and Pete would be at the selected spots. Uncle Fred, Dad, and I left the cabin and began the chase about an hour after Uncle Rudy, and Pete had started. Uncle Rudy had his 300 Savage and Dad carried the old lever action 40.82. (40 caliber designed in 1882). I again carried the 30.30. Shortly after we left camp, Uncle Fred again took a different trail and Dad and I advanced up the valley.

Just before sunup, off in the distance, Dad spotted something moving. Dad quickly lied down on the cold ground and pulled me down with him. He pointed to the hillside above us but I didn't see anything. Then, there it was. I saw what looked like large dead tree branches moving. Under these branches (antlers) was the head of an immense bull elk. The elk came over the hill and started down toward us. It just kept coming.

At about 100 yards away, it stopped, turned to its right and began running along the hillside. Dad aimed and squeezed the trigger. There was a large blast and a flame from the barrel of the old 40.82. Dad had missed. You could see where the bullet hit the hillside several feet below the big elk. He fired again. This time holding the sights several feet over the large shoulder of the bull elk. The elk fell.

      He tried to get up but couldn't. Dad and I walked up the hill toward the elk keeping several yards distance from him. The elk was pawing at the ground with his hooves and shaking his head while making snorting sounds. His back was broken and he could only drag his rear quarters. We worked our way above the area where the elk was struggling. Dad took the 30.30 that I was carrying and shot it behind the ear. The big bull dropped dead. It was a magnificent six point bull elk - that is, six points on each side.

      With caution, Dad walked toward the elk and once by his side proceeded to cut the elk's throat. Dad thrust the knife downward sharply and failed to stop it before it sliced through his left boot and into his large toe. Dad removed his boot and saw that the wound was bleeding and was very deep. Today we would rush to the emergency room for stitches. But Dad wrapped the wound with his hanky and put his bloody sock and boot back on. He took the 30.30 and fired three blasts into the air. He wanted to save the few 40.82 bullets he had left, knowing that they were getting scarce. I think they were no longer available in any of the local stores. Dad cleaned the elk while we waited for the other hunters to arrive.

      Since the cabin was down hill from where the elk was killed, everyone agreed that dragging the elk intact would be better than quartering it. The head was removed and the stomach opening was stitched closed to keep it clean. With ropes tied to the legs, the task of getting the big elk down to the cabin began. The men towed the elk and I again had the liver and heart in my knapsack. This time I also had the head and horns. I wasn't going to give up that trophy. However, I didn't realize how heavy the trophy was and, just as I was about to give in, we stopped to rest and saw some hunters on horseback riding up the valley toward us. They stopped to admire the kill and offered to drag the elk back to camp for us. We didn't turn them down. This group of hunters was the Spehar party. Dad called one of them "Father Spehar" and I asked Dad why he called the man "father." Dad said, "Because he is a Father, a Catholic priest." Until that time, I didn't know that priests hunted.

The elk's rear legs were tied to a long rope, which was then wrapped around the saddle-horn of a large horse. The horse was spooked and didn't like the elk. It reared up and started to run but when the rope became taut the horse was jerked backward and his run slowed considerably. Dragging the elk down the valley the horse still moved too fast for us to keep up. As we ran the men gave me a hand carrying the head and antlers. When we got to the cabin, we saw the horse with the elk. It had stopped at the barbed-wire fence near the cabin, still unhappy about being tied to the big elk.

LEFT: Unknown hunter and Grandpa Naglich, early 1930's.

BELOW: The writer with an elk killed by his dad in 1943.

With two large elk to share, the hunt was a great success, so it was decided that we would return to Crested Butte in the morning. Ruda started dinner and the men passed the whiskey bottle around several times. Dad removed his boot and the severed toe looked pretty bad. He cleaned his foot with cold water, poured some whiskey on the wound and put on a clean heavy white sock. He didn't waste much whiskey on the toe.

In the morning, we woke to a light snow. It was time to leave. We loaded the elk and remaining supplies into the dump truck and left just as the snow began coming down in large flakes.

When we got to Crested Butte, the word about our success spread quickly and many friends came see and admire our trophies. A single elk kill was big news in our town and to come home with two large elk was a rarity.

Like the Indians before us, once the meat was divided it was turned over to the women folk. Mom began carving away and, except for a few steaks that she stored in the small refrigerator, she cooked and canned the rest, storing it in the cellar for future use. It was still too early in the year for a hard freeze so canning was the method used to preserve the meat.

Oh, by the way, Dad walked with a limp for several days but his toe healed with almost no remaining scar. I don't know if it was the whiskey or the heavy white sock.

The following year we were invited to go hunting on opening day of the season at great Uncle George Volk's ranch up the Muddy (Ragged Mountain). We had the same hunters from the great hunt of '43 except for Ruda Sporcich, who didn't accompany us. We arrived at the ranch early evening the day before the hunt.

The Volk boys (men) had all the scouting pre-arranged for us and we started early the next day. The hunt was very different from the year before. We soon found out why they called it Ragged Mountain. The hills were covered with low-lying brush that tore at our clothes and at times forced us to crawl on our knees. If we saw an opening it was small and covered with tall grass. We could hear and sometimes see game running ahead of us, but never long enough to get our sights on it.

After two days of "hide and seek", we headed home. The only shots fired were the ones from a member of the hunting party who got lost, so that he could be located.

On the road that evening, the fuel pump on Dad's '39 Chrysler quit about a mile west of Kebler Pass summit. Dad removed the gas cap and blew into the tank several times forcing fuel to the carburetor. He started the car and we headed on up again. He had to repeat this procedure two or three more times before we made it to the summit but once we got there and headed down hill with gravity the fuel could run down to the carburetor and the problem was solved. We were all glad to see the lights of Crested Butte. Dad put his "X" on hunting up the Muddy. This was 1944 and my last hunt in the Crested Butte area.

I can't close this chapter on hunting in Crested Butte without making mention of the greatest hunter ever from this small mountain town, John Plute. The following was extracted from old issues of the Crested Butte Pilot and Chronicle, the Empire Magazine and Outdoor Life. In all cases, the articles used the caveat, "to the best of our knowledge."

John Plute was a very tall dishwater blond coalminer who loved horses, hunting, gambling, and drinking. There were locals in Crested Butte who said that he was a hunting guide for President Teddy Roosevelt when the he was hunting in the Crested Butte area. John was given the nickname "O Bog, O Bog," meaning "Oh God, oh God" in Croatian. They called him that because he often said, "Oh Bog, Oh Bog," when he talked.

In 1899 O Bog, O Bog was hunting in Dark Canyon west of Crested Butte when he spotted a huge elk and leveled his rifle. The elk filled the open sights of his .30/40 Krag. He squeezed the trigger and the huge elk fell. Normally John would have only kept the meat from his kill, but the antlers were so large John carried them home. He proudly displayed these enormous horns to his friends. The antlers were stored in a friend's garage until 1915 when he traded them to John Rozich for his rather large bar bill. The antlers were displayed on the wall of Rozich Bar, later the Rozeman Bar for several years.

His love for wild horses and whiskey ended in his demise. In 1922 John left a picnic at the Malensek Ranch for a ride on his bronc. He never returned to the picnic. Rudy Malensek went looking for him and found him a short distance away. He had been thrown from his horse and his head struck some rocks. He was taken to Gunnison hospital and died five days later.

Research of his death at a later date found a death certificate for a John Pluth (note spelling). The record stated, "John Pluth born of Austrian parents in 1868 died October 10, 1922." Cause of death was listed as, clot at the base of the brain, caused from falling off a horse. He was 54 years old. No one questioned the death certificate. His name was just misspelled.

Sixty-two years after John killed that huge elk and 39 years after his death it was recorded and certified by the Boone & Crocket Club as the largest ever killed.

John Plute died like he lived. The burial of his remains is a mystery. A search of the local cemeteries found no tombstone for John Plute. No one knows what happened to the remains of O Bog, O Bog.

CHAPTER 7: SPORTS & GAMES

MARBLES

The snow has melted in the streets but it is still piled in the yards in areas that see little sunshine. The water in Coal Creek is roaring and thrashing against its banks. The city has removed the boxed enclosures of manure from around all of the fire hydrants. (In early winter a wooden box enclosure is built around each fire hydrant and filled with manure from the mule barn to keep the water hydrants from freezing during the very cold winter). These are the first signs of spring. It is marble season!

Every boy in town played marbles. As we walked or ran, you could see the bulges in their pockets and hear the click of loose marbles striking each other. We were either looking for a game or already playing. We didn't have to go far to find a game. Marble players were like professional boxers - always wanting to challenge the champ. If you were good at marbles, your reputation developed in a very short time. The games were either funzies or keepers. In funzies we always returned our winnings to the boy who lost them but in keepers we kept all of the marbles that we won. If another player challenged us and our reputation was at stake, the game was played for keeps. There were many games played with marbles, but we stuck to three basic ones: Poison, Mibs (regular marbles), or Bullring. Usually a challenge for your reputation was Bullring. In Poison we dug four holes in the dirt about the size of a tuna can. Three of the holes were in line about eight feet apart and the fourth hole (poison hole) was offset about the same distance. The game was played very much like croquet. Each player in turn lagged or shot his marble from hole to hole until he reached the poison hole. If he rolled his marble into a hole or struck another players marble he got another turn. If he didn't the next player in line took his turn. However, if another marble struck his before he reached the poison hole, he had to start over again. If a marble that had reached the poison hole struck his marble, he was out of the game and had to surrender his marble.

Regular marbles (Mibs) started with each player placing a like amount of marbles in a football shaped ring scribed in the ground. The number of marbles each player placed in the ring depended on the number of players. Usually each player placed one to five marbles in the ring. Than each would lag for a line several feet away. The player who owned the marble closest to the line would be first. He would lag his taw (prized shooter) back toward the football shaped ring trying to knock a marble out of the ring. He continued shooting as long as he didn't miss knocking a marble out of the ring. If he missed, it was the next player's turn, and his taw remained where it came to rest as a target for the other players. As the shooter, you could choose to shoot a marble out of the ring or to shoot at another player's taw. If you hit another player's taw, he was out of the game. When it was your turn again, you had to shoot from the place your taw landed on your last shot. Play continued until all of the marbles were knocked out of the ring, or until only one player remained in the game.

In Bullring, the players scribed a ring in the ground of about four to six feet in diameter and each placed a like number of marbles in the ring. As in Mibs, all the players would lag to a line some distance away to see who would start the game. The closest to the line was first. In this game, the first shooter started by shooting his taw from the outside perimeter of the large ring toward a marble. If he hit and knocked a marble out of the ring, he would continue to shoot his taw from the position where it last rested in the ring. He remained the shooter as long as he continued knocking a marble or marbles out of the ring. If his taw glanced out of the ring when he knocked a marble out of it, he would continue shooting but would have to start from the outside of the perimeter again. If he missed a marble on any shot and his taw remained in the ring, it was fair game for the next shooter. If he missed a marble during the shot and his taw rolled out of the ring, he picked up his taw and waited for his turn again. The game ended when all of the marbles were knocked out of the bullring or one of the players won all of the other players' taws.

There were several variations to all marble games, and the rules of the game were discussed and agreed upon by all of the players before the first taw was shot.

We played with several different types of marbles. Most were machine-made, but we often saw the older handmade marbles. Some of those handmade were clay and called "chinkies." Glazed marbles were called "pot eyes;" agates, called "aggies;" and glass marbles, called "swirls," "ribbons," "clams," "onion skins" and "clearies."

Most machine-made marbles were glass and were called "slags, "swirls," "opaques," "corkscrews," "rainbows," "cat eyes" and other. The "steelie" was another very common machine-made marble, which was one of the balls removed from the race of a ball bearing. "Steelies" came in many sizes, but glass marble sizes were pretty standard. Most glass marbles were 5/8 inches or ¾ inches in diameter. My favorite taw was a ¾-inch "aggie" that my Dad bought for me at a gift shop in Colorado Springs. We had to break in a taw, just like you had to break in a good baseball glove. If a taw had a smooth, glossy surface it was hard to hold on your thumb knuckle. We would shoot it against other marbles until its surface became somewhat less than smooth and therefore "broken in".

The proper shooting position was with your taw held on your thumb knuckle by the tip of your index finger and resting on the topside of your middle finger. The taw was propelled with great force by flicking your thumb forward. Some of the younger players placed their taw low on their thumbnail. We'd laugh and tease them and call them names. Some players pushed their hand forward as they released their taw. This was called "fudging," and they were penalized.

The equipment for marbles was minimal. All you needed was marbles. Extras, and nice to have, were a draw string bag in which to carry your marbles and a pad to protect your knuckles. After the first few days of marble season, my knuckles would bleed. Mom would have me soak my hand in salt water and at night she would rub Cloverine Salve on my knuckles. Mom made a pad to protect my knuckles. It was a round piece of sheepskin with the hide side out and it worked so well that she ended up making them for several of my friends.

If you had a good day at marbles, you skipped home with a smile and both pockets bulging with clicking marbles. A bad day was a slow walk home, no smile, and no noise coming from your pockets.

OTHER SUMMER FUN

At almost 9000 feet in altitude, it didn't take long for the hot sun to melt the winter's snow and dry out the mud holes. By midsummer, all of us kids were thinking of things like fishing, hunting, building a cabin or fort, playing baseball and swimming.

The men in town usually had a baseball team, but in those years, when I was playing baseball with my friends, most of them were in Europe or in the Pacific fighting the war. There, also, weren't enough kids in Crested Butte to make two full baseball teams but we would gather as many as we could and go to the ball diamond to play a modified baseball game. We usually had enough to play Workups or Out and Back.

Workups was not a team game. We usually had a batter, catcher, pitcher and fielders. The batter remained the batter until he made an out by striking out or flying out to another player. When the batter struck out, everyone would move up one position and the batter would take his place in the field. If the batter would fly out he would change positions with the player who caught the ball.

Out and Back was a team game played like baseball except we only used first base. When the batter hit the ball he had to run to first base and return to home. The batter could make an out by striking out, hitting a fly ball, which was caught by another player or by not being able to run to first base and back to home plate before the ball was thrown to the catcher at home plate.

Like marbles, there were many variations to these games and the rules had to be agreed upon before each game. Even with these discussions, arguments still persisted and additional rules had to be agreed upon. No matter how aggressive the arguments were, we all went home joking and remaining the best of friends.

In the afternoons it was usually time to cool off. We would head for one of the swimming holes; either the Volk's on a bend in Coal Creek, about a quarter mile from the cemetery bridge, Gully, a bend in Slate river off of the Peanut Mine road about a mile from the city limit sign or Nickelson's Lake. We didn't go to the lake very often, as it was a four mile walk. Volk's was only four or five feet deep at the bend but Gully was larger and deeper. It was also much colder. Before arriving at the swimming hole, each of us would gather a large bundle of firewood, old dry willows or an old tire. This was our "share". A "share" was required if you were going to swim. First, we started a large fire and everyone gathered around it telling stories or the latest gossip in town. This is where most of us boys learned about the "birds and the bees." When someone got the nerve to dive into the cold water everyone else followed. No one stayed in very long though and soon we were all back around the fire shivering with goose bumps all over our bodies and our teeth chattering behind our purple lips. O yes! Swimming was a "boys only" sport as no one wore or owned swim trunks.

Often we played "cops and robbers" with rubber-guns. They were of wood constructed into a pistol shape with a clothespin for a trigger, which was mounted on the rear of the pistol grip with a rubber band. The rubber bands, which were also used as ammunition, were cut from automobile inner tubes. Before World War II inner tubes were made from natural rubber and were very elastic. To load the gun, we would stick one end of a rubber band into the jaws of the clothespin and stretch the other end of it over the barrel of the gun. We would always tie the rubber band in a knot first to give it more force and distance. To fire the projectile (rubber band) we would then just squeeze the clothespin.

We would also choose teams. One team would hide and the other would hunt them down. Once hit by a rubber band, you were out of the game. Our favorite place to play cops and robbers was a vacant two-story house and an ice shed on First Street, just a block from the Big Mine Tipple.

In the evening, before curfew, we always played games. This was one time the boys and girls played together. We played tag and two variations of hide and seek; "run sheep, run" and "kick the can."

In "kick the can," when we wanted everyone to return to the can, we would yell, "Ollie, ollie oxen free." I could never figure out what this beast of burden had to do with getting everyone back until several years later when I found out that it was appropriately, "All ye, all ye still out can come in free."

WINTER GAMES

SKIING

Gosh, summer went by fast. It's fall already. Time for school, big game hunting and the first snow fall. It seems like only yesterday that we were swimming in Coal Creek.

It seemed like the first snowfall never stopped. Winter was here, and both kids and grownups were ready to take advantage of the snow; skiing, sled riding, tobogganing, ice-skating, and late winter crust walking.

Just as it is today, skiing was going down a hill on a pair of boards strapped to your feet. The difference is that the boards and straps have changed immensely from the flat-tip pine boards with a slot cut through center for an adjustable leather strap, which tightened over the toe of our rubber over shoes. Our boots were held in the leather strap with a heavy rubber band that was cut from an automobile inner tube. We placed the rubber band around our ankle before we placed our over boot into the strap of our ski. Then we took the rubber band and stretched it over our toe, adjusted it and pulled it down on the back of the heel. Not quite as good as the bindings of today, but it kept our skis from beating us down the hill.

When I was seven or eight years old, Mom and Dad bought me a pair of maple ridge top skis, five and a half feet long. Everything was in feet and inches at that time. We didn't know what a centimeter was. The best skis you could buy were laminated hickory with metal edges and a ridge top. The size was determined by your height.

To properly measure for a slalom ski, we would stand up straight, raise our arms above our heads, and measure the distance from the floor to the center of our hand. Properly fitted, the skis were much longer than the slalom skis of today. My five foot, six inch skis were a bit long for me when I got them, but like my pants, I would grow into them. These skis had leather bindings that were actually screwed on. Santa was good that year. I also got my first pair of ski poles, which were made of bamboo. With this semi-modern equipment, I could out ski all of my friends.

The following Christmas, Santa brought me a pair of ski boots and a modification kit to change my leather bindings to spring and cable. No one my age could beat me on the slopes now. The ski boots were very different than those of today. They were low cut like the cross-country boots of today, however they were made of leather not a man-made material. They had a metal strip on the sole in front of the boot that locked into the front of the binding and groove cut into the heel that fit into a spring cable. With just a forward thrust of the latch, you were locked into your skis.

Christmas Eve, I wore my boots to Midnight Mass and I wasn't alone. I noticed a few of the other kids were wearing new ski boots when they received Communion. Not only did we wear our boots for skiing, we also wore them to school when the season was over. Even though they were very large when we first put them on, they wouldn't fit a growing boy the next ski season.

Somewhere around this same time, I got my first pair of ski pants. They were baggy, made of wool gabardine with an elastic strap on the bottom of the legs, which went around the arch of my foot. A pair of suspenders held up the ski pants. This was the first time I skied that my stockings didn't show as they were worn under the ski pants. Before ski pants, we always wore wool stockings over our regular pants, held up with a rubber band. The rest of my ski equipment and attire was a pair of ski goggles, long ski mittens, Mom's white wool shawl-collared sweater, and her wine-colored tam with a pheasant feather.

The only commercial ski resort in the Crested Butte area was the Pioneer. It was located about three miles north on the Cement Creek Canyon road and had three ski runs, a chair lift, and a rope tow. The Big Dipper, Little Dipper and the Milky Way were the names of the three runs. The chair lift took us to the top of the Big Dipper and near the top of the Little Dipper. The rope tow was on the Milky Way. In the 40s, when it opened, it only operated on weekends. I skied Pioneer only once when Dad took Uncle Jake and me.

All of our skiing otherwise, was done in and around Crested Butte where we built our own runs and jumps. We packed and skied a run on Chocolate Peak starting at the top and skiing down the steep slope to the Coal Creek Bridge on First Street. We packed all of the eastside of the hill and had several trails and a jump. Malensick's Hill was also made into a very popular area to ski. We always had a large run from the Aspen trees on the top of the hill ending just north of the large barn and rock wall, before the tall barbed wire fence. We also packed a ski area and made a large jump on Pueblo Mine Hill.

There were rules for skiing just as there were for marbles and swimming. The first rule was that before you skied down the slope, it was necessary to pack it. This was done by all of the skiers side stepping their skies up the hill in a method we called the "step ladder." There weren't any tows on these courses anyway so as we climbed the hill we packed the snow. After a few climbs, the course began to take shape. Once the trail was packed, we could climb the trail with a step called the "herringbone" which was accomplished by taking "V" steps with the tips of our skis pointed out and upward. The herringbone was a much faster method of climbing up the slope provided the snow was packed and hill was not too steep. If the slope was steep, you reverted to the step ladder approach.

There was also a rule about filling your hole. If anyone fell on the course, it usually made a large "divot" which had to be filled in with snow and packed even with the surrounding run. Leaving a divot unfilled and unpacked was dangerous to the skiers following you down the same hill.

After several trips packing up hill and skiing down, it was time to go home. While cross-country skiing home, we talked about our skiing plans for the next day hoping that the long night wouldn't bring too much new snow so that we could do more skiing than packing.

There were several other areas in which to ski --- Chicken Ranch, Red Lady, and Smith Hill. However, we pre-teeners stayed near home, as the other areas were historically known to have avalanches.

SKATING

In the winter months besides skiing we also ice-skated and like skiing, it was work before play. First we needed to shovel the snow off of the frozen frog ponds that were near the railroad depot. If the snow was not deep, we could clear the ice pretty quickly by skating and pushing the shovel in front of us like a snowplow. With several skaters, each pushing a number-two coal shovel, we could clear the pond in a short time. In the meantime we also built a bonfire where we could warm up after we had finished.

When all of the work was done we played hockey or just skated for fun. Most of us had clip-on skates that fastened to our boots and it wasn't until later on that we had shoe skates. They were a low-cut hockey-type skate and were quite an advantage over the clip-ons that came off of our feet quite easily and needed constant attention.

Besides the frozen ponds we skated at Peanut Lake, but it was a much farther walk from town. By the time we cleared a skating area, it was time to come home. However when cleared the ice on Peanut Lake was like glass and worth the extra walk.

SLEDDING

Almost every kid in Crested Butte owned a sled with a wooden bed bolted to a metal frame with metal runners and a wooden steering bar up front. When pressure was applied to one side of the steering bar, the steel runners would warp and give some steering capability. This, along with a lot of body language, allowed you to make a shallow turn.

The best sled run in Crested Butte was on the road from Chocolate Peak down Elk Avenue. At that time, the highway to Kebler Pass went west on Elk Avenue and southwest to Chocolate Peak. It was closed to vehicles during the winter, and there was very little automobile traffic on the streets in Crested Butte. When the sled trail was packed, became firm and iced over, we had a great run starting near the top of Chocolate Peak and heading down Elk Avenue all the way to the Princess Theater. Anything beyond the City Hall was a good run.

With our sled held at our side we would run as fast as we could and then jump on our sled belly-buster style. Once we got our composure, we prepared for our first turn. The last and hardest turn to negotiate was the right turn onto Elk Avenue. We were at top speed going into it and if our timing was off we would lose speed, or worse, have to roll off of our sled in order to keep from running into one of the houses near the turn. Winning was not the best time, but the best distance.

TOBOGGANING

I was only five years old when the ski and toboggan run was built, from the top of Slobodnik's Hill and down Elk Avenue, by the Gallowich brothers and several others. It was 1938, a year of record snowfall. The run was very steep, hard packed with steep sides to keep us on the course and a snow tunnel at the top. We had to stay really low on our skis to make it through the tunnel.

The steep run was also used for toboggans, which are long flat sleds without runners. A toboggan was made of wood with the front curled upward so it could coast on the snow. It was about eight feet long and usually could carry three or four riders. On the upper surface of the wooden toboggan, running lengthwise on both sides was a rope, which gave you something to hold onto while gliding down a slope. Each rider would sit on the toboggan and place his or her feet on the lap of the rider in front of them. The last rider in the back would run, pushing the toboggan to get it started and then jump on and assume the same sitting position.

Total control of the toboggan was by holding onto the ropes and leaning as a team. The last man on was usually the leader and would yell, "left" or "right." Working together, you could make a slight direction change. With the sloped steep sides of the run, and working as a team, the run was usually made without a mishap. Like the contest on a sled, greatest distance down the hill was the objective. To give more speed and distance, the toboggans, like skis, had the running surface waxed with beeswax.

There were only a few toboggans in town and my Dad built the best ones. He made me a small toboggan. It was five feet long with the front curl made from heavy tin over a wooden form. I used my toboggan for going down the hill in front of the house, but never in competition with the big toboggans that went down Slobodnik's Hill.

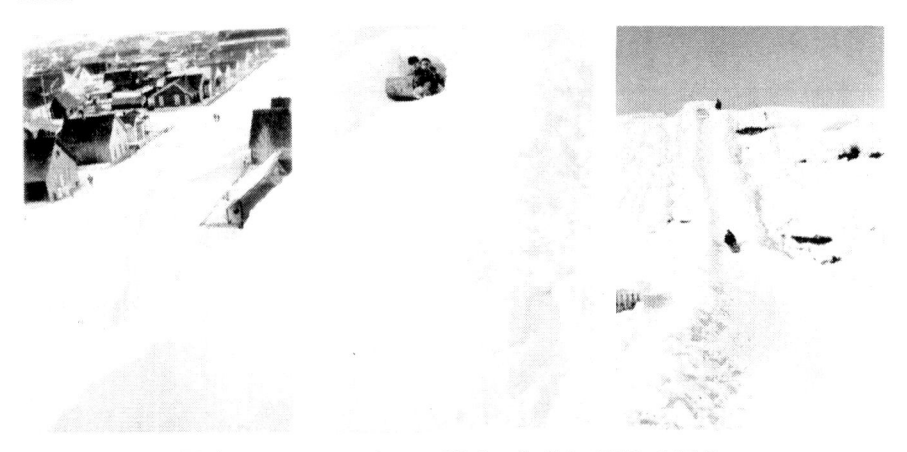

Toboggan run down Slobodnik's Hill, 1938.

CRUST WALKING

In late winter, Mom and Dad used to go crust walking. The surface of the snow would melt during the day and refreeze during the night. In the early morning they could walk on the crusted snow without breaking the surface and would pull me behind them in my toboggan. These walks were usually not very long as shortly after the sun came up and heated the snow, they would sink with every step. The crust walks were always a great way to start the weekend.

ABOVE LEFT: 1935 – The writer with his sled.
ABOVE RIGHT: Writer and his mother.
BELOW LEFT: 1920's – Mother and Aunt Rose.
BELOW RIGHT: Mom and Dad.

CHAPTER 8: THE MOST UNFORGETTABLE CHARACTERS

PEANUTS

When I think about the many times I walked with my friends to one of our swimming holes, I think about my little ball and chain, and how I tried everything to get rid of him. My ball and chain was my cousin Rudy Kochevar Junior. Although his given name was Rudolph, family called him Junior and everyone else called him Peanuts. I have been told that I gave him the nickname Peanuts and I possibly did, but I don't remember the occasion.

Rudy, Junior, Peanuts is six years younger than me and was the first-born to Uncle Rudy and Aunt Margaret. As a baby, he was cute but not beautiful. He was skinny, had knobby knees and protruding ears. He also had a big smile, and his eyes had a special twinkle.

Shortly after Peanuts learned to walk, he found that his house and yard were not large enough for him and he began to wonder off. To prohibit this from happening Uncle Rudy locked all the gates including ours. We had adjoining yards with no fence between them. This worked for a year or so, and then Peanuts learned to climb over the fence. Once over, he was gone. Usually he set out looking for me but if I was nowhere to be found he would just wonder around downtown Crested Butte. Aunt Margaret didn't know what to do. Peanuts was not going to stay in the house, or the yard for that matter. Finally Aunt Margaret decided she would dress him in girls' clothes thinking that he would be too embarrassed to leave the house. Peanuts made a pretty cute looking girl when wearing his dress. To Auntie's surprise, this didn't stop Peanuts. He just picked up his skirt so that he could run fast, and he was on his way.

Uncle Rudy's next idea was to string barbed wire on the top of the fences surrounding both our yards with a double row of barbed wire on top of the back fence that bordered Coal Creek and back yards. This seemed to be the answer, at least for a while. The only one who ever got hurt on the barbed wire was me.

Everyone used Coal Creek as a disposal for everything. Because the fence was high, Mom and I needed a bench to stand on in order to throw anything over it and into the creek. One winter morning, I was throwing the ashes from the stove over the back fence and a leg on the bench broke. I slipped on the icy surface and ended up hanging from the barbed wire. The barbs held my left arm, and I couldn't get loose nor could I get my footing on the icy bench. I yelled and yelled. Mom finally came and freed me from the fence and treated my wounds.

As Peanuts grew a little older, he also grew wiser. He learned how to properly place his hands and feet on the barbed wire and he was off a gain.

As I mentioned earlier, if Peanuts couldn't find me, he just wandered on the main street. About this time, he also picked up another habit. He started smoking cigarette butts that he would find as he was walking the street.

Uncle Rudy came up with yet another idea of how to keep Peanuts in the yard. He found an eight-inch cast-iron pipe elbow at the Big Mine, and he brought it home. He attached the cast-iron elbow to one end of a ten-foot long chain and Peanut's ankle to the other. This cast iron elbow weighed over ten pounds. Peanuts learned that he could pick up the heavy elbow, walk to the fence, throw the elbow over the fence and then carefully maneuver himself over the barbed wire. Once over the fence, he would pick up the cast iron elbow, hold it with both hands and head for town.

The last method Uncle Rudy tried worked. Using the same ten-foot chain he hooked one end to Peanut's ankle and the other to a large post that supported the second story porch of the house. Uncle Rudy won. Peanuts could no longer run away.

After years of running away from Peanuts, and even throwing rocks at him to keep him from following me, I gave in. He now became my responsibility. I would unhook him from the post and my little ball and chain would tag along with me to the swimming hole or wherever I went.

Peanut's fifth birthday is a story in itself. As I mentioned earlier, he had taken up smoking and would often steal cigarettes from Uncle Fred. On his birthday, he wanted to smoke so Uncle Rudy bought corncob pipes for him and cousin, John Michael Spritzer. Next he took Grandpa Kochevar's humidor from behind the old bar. Grandpa Kochevar wasn't very selective in his choice of tobacco and the humidor only contained Prince Albert and many old cigar butts that he had chopped up. Peanuts and John Michael (Spike) proudly filled their corncob pipes to the brim with Grandpa's tobacco. Uncle Rudy held the match. I don't remember how many pipes full the cousins smoked, but Uncle Rudy just laughed and egged them on. I remember both of them turning green and getting sick. It was a lesson learned. I think it was over a week before Peanuts picked up another butt again.

As Peanuts grew up he became quite agile and muscular, excelling in all sports and playing a great trumpet. It was exciting and somewhat amazing to see the knobby-kneed boy with the special glitter in his eyes become a handsome family man and educator. Peanuts, also, still maintains a single digit golf handicap.

OTHERS

The following are only a few of the many unforgettable characters I knew or heard about while living in Crested Butte. Many of the others are mentioned in other parts of this book.

BILL (KVATERNICK) TEZAK (WUBBS)

In 1939 Billy Tezak (not the same as Uncle Bill Tezak) and I started school together in Crested Butte and became very good friends. His father, Mark Tezak died when Bill was just a few years old and so he was raised by his mother and grandmother, Mrs. Kvaternick. Since his Grandmother never spoke English, Billy spoke Slovenian as his first language. Being raised by two women Billy had to learn all of the boy and man things for himself.

During the summer months, we spent many days playing cops and robbers in both an old deserted house and the icehouse located on First Street between Sopris Avenue and White Rock Avenue. We would divide into two teams, the hunters and the hunted. Oh yes, we did have weapons --- rubber guns.

As I mentioned before, Billy was raised by two protective women and had to make his own crude rubber guns. He always played, but was usually the last one selected on a team because he was very shy and his rubber guns lacked the power of the other players guns.

One day, in the heat of a gun battle, Billy was shot in the face with a very strongly knotted rubber. He cried out, "I got shot with a wubber. I got shot in the eye with a wubber." Still crying, Billy ran down the alley and all the way to his house. From that day on no one ever called him Billy. He was "Wubbs."

Wubbs first love was fishing and whenever he could get away from home you could find him out fishing. One day, while still grade school age, he went fishing in Coal Creek under the bridge on Elk Avenue. He cast his bait, felt a tug on the line and the fight was on. Wubbs caught and landed a two-pounder. That was the largest fish that I can remember ever being taken from Coal Creek.

I lost track of Wubbs for a long time until I saw he and his lovely wife Clyeda at the Crested Butte Reunion in 1999. We hugged and reminisced about old times.

CHARLIE MARKOVICH

Charlie was an emigrant coalminer, who came to Crested Butte from the "Old Country," (Slovenia). He came as a single man and from his habits he was destined to stay that way. He lived in the log cabin behind the Kochevar house that Mom, Dad, and I had lived in prior to Charlie and is now the restaurant "The Soupcon." The total atmosphere of the cabin changed when Charlie moved in. He never believed in the saying, "Cleanliness is next to Godliness." He, also, always kept a crock of sauerkraut and had stale sausage and smoked meat hung from the rafters of his enclosed front porch.

One of the stories told about was that one morning while frying eggs on his old coal stove, he noticed a mouse in his frying pan. He picked the mouse out from the eggs, tossed it to the cat outside and continued frying his eggs.

Grandma often complained to Charlie about the condition of the cabin and once threatened to move him out. Charlie's response was that if she had any complaints she should talk to her daughter, Carolyn (my Mom), since, he said, it was in the same condition when he moved in.

Charlie's attire was much like his house. He had bib overalls and other work clothes that he left at the mine and another pair with a shirt and other scant attire that he wore the rest of the time. The only time any of his clothes were ever washed was when Grandma Kochevar insisted that he bring them over to the big house where she would soak them in hot soapy water for a long time and then attempt to scrub them clean.

My Dad told me this story many years ago.

After Charlie had gotten drunk at one of the many saloons in Crested Butte, some of his friends, Rudy Saya, Charlie Songer, and I think my Dad, dragged him to his log cabin. At that time the sidewalks on Elk Avenue were wooden, and Charlie got several splinters in his rear end. When he mentioned that he had a sore rear end to his "buddies," they laid him on his bed, removed his overalls, found a pair of pliers and began to operate.

When they jerked out the first splinter, Charlie screamed, "Oh my Jesus, Oh my Jesus." His buddies laughed and continued the operation. Charlie shouted this same phrase with every jerk of the pliers. Several of the jerks were not splinters but hair from Charlie's rear end. By the time the last splinter was removed, his rear end was tweezed bald.

Uncle John Spritzer told the story, that once when he and Charlie were walking home from the mine, they saw a dead groundhog lying in the street. Charlie picked up the groundhog, put it in his jacket pocket and told Uncle John that it would be his dinner for that night.

In 1943, when I was living with Grandma, Charlie came to the back door and asked if I could help him cut some logs, which he needed for the following winter. He said he would pay me two dollars a day. The downed trees were near Slate River south of the Smith Hill mine. Grandma said I could go, and early the next morning I met Charlie at his house. He had a two-bladed ax and a long two-handled logging saw.

Charlie put the lunch that Grandma had made for us in his pack and carried the long wobbly saw. I carried the ax. We walked the road to Peanut mine and then up the old railroad bed to the fallen trees. I think they now call this route the lower loop. When we got to our destination we had to forge the river to get to the fallen trees. We proceeded to remove our shoes and socks---well, at least, I removed my shoes and socks. Charlie removed his steel-toed shoes and large squares of burlap that covered each of his feet.

When we got to the other side of the river, and began to put our shoes back on I watched Charlie. He dried his feet on his pant leg and placed one of his feet in the center of the burlap square. He wrapped the burlap up both sides of his foot, folded it over his toes and heel and slipped his foot into his shoe.

Charlie used the ax to cut the branches from the fallen logs and I carried the branches up river, out of our way. Once the trees were cleaned of their branches, we proceeded to cut the tree into logs about 14 inches long --- just the size to make kindling for the winter. We worked all day, stopping only for lunch. In the late afternoon we started the long walk home and arrived just before sundown. We repeated this logging task for two more weekends. On Sunday we started a little later in the day as I had to attend early Mass.

At the end of the second Sunday, we had all of the logs cut into kindling size and stacked near the river. Charlie's plan was to float the logs down the river the next weekend and retrieve them at the cemetery bridge.

The next weekend, when Charlie got to the place where we had left the logs, he found that they had disappeared. Someone had stolen all of the logs. Charlie was heartbroken, as he had promised half of the logs to Tony Verzuh.

This bachelor life finally got the best of my friend Charlie. Several years after the logging incident he was placed in the State Hospital in Pueblo where he remained until his death.

OGDEN/LOGAN (THE GARDENER)

Around 1913 or 1914, before my Dad started school, there lived an old gentleman who raised vegetables and peddled them to the women in Crested Butte. Dad said his name was Logan, John Spritzer remembers it as Ogden. Whatever his name, he deserves a few lines in this book.

The Gardener raised vegetables on Slobodnik's hill. For those of you not acquainted with Slobodnik's hill, if you walked west as far as you could go on Elk Avenue and then climbed the hill to the top, you would be at Slobodniks. Years ago there were wooden steps from the end of Elk Avenue to the top of the hill. As kids, we played on them counting them as we went. Today all I can remember is that there were many and we rested several times before we made it to Slobodniks.

The Gardener would make this trip down the hill with a large basket strapped to his back. Dad said he would always walk down the hill backwards. He would walk the neighborhood and sell his vegetables daily. Dad said that Grandma would wait for him to get to First Street, his first stop, and always buy some of his fresh vegetables. After The Gardener sold his vegetables, he would buy what he needed at a local store and return up the many steps to his garden and cabin.

Walking these many steps would have been a chore for most anyone, but more so for Ogden/Logan The Gardener as he had had both legs amputated above the knee and had only heavy leather pads attached to what remained of his legs.

JOHN POBRIK

Like many emigrants from the "old country," John Pobrik worked hard and drank hard. He was a miner in the winter and ran a sawmill in the summer that was located west of Crested Butte about two or three miles east of Kebler Pass. John had a wife, a daughter whose name was Evelyn and two sons, Herman and Billy. Herman was my age and Billy was younger.

The first time I met Mr. Pobrik I was with Dad on the bulldozer bucking snow on Elk Avenue. The Pobriks lived on the eastside of Elk Avenue near the railroad station. When Dad was plowing snow next to Mr. Pobrik's house he came running out and asked Dad if he would push the snow out of his driveway. Dad obliged and Mr. Pobrik brought a bottle of whiskey from the house from which he and Dad took a large slug. I can still picture this thin man in overalls telling Dad in broken English, "Janco, me thank you. This summer ve avah pachin in Gothic. You bring lamb, I bring vine and ve avah ellova time." He again thanked dad and went into the house.

Dad told me that he was over the Pobrik house once when Herman hadn't completed his chores. When Mr. Pobrik found that the chores were not completed, this domineering man called, "Erman, get mein razor strop and come to the coal shed, where you and me gonna dance the two step."

I don't know why these incidents and this man are still so vivid in my mind unless they all depicted the hard but colorful life of so many I remember while growing up in Crested Butte.

CHAPTER 9: SCHOOL & CHURCH

SCHOOL

As mentioned in an earlier chapter, life in the town of Crested Butte centered around The Company. This was true, but it also evolved around our school and our churches.

I started school in Crested Butte at the age of six when I entered the first grade. There was no kindergarten or preschool. I was there for my first, second, third, and fifth grades and was taught by Mrs. Kohn, Baggete, Starkovich, and Meack. My fourth, sixth, and subsequent grades were completed in Pueblo, Colorado. I spent the summer before my fifth grade in Crested Butte, and didn't want to return to Pueblo. I pleaded with Mom and Dad to let me stay in Crested Butte and after many promises, they agreed to let me live there with Grandma and Grandpa Kochevar for a year.

Grandma and I struck a bargain. I was to teach Grandma how to write in English, and she was to teach me to speak in Slovenian. Before the year was out, Grandma was writing to my Mom in English but my Slovenian remained very limited. I did learn the names of all of the foods on the dinner table, as I didn't get seconds unless I asked for them in Slovenian.

Not only did we learn the three R's in the first grade we had to learn a lot more - like how to get along with our other classmates. Before we started school, we only knew and played with relatives.

School was also where we encountered flushable toilets. They were the gravity types, with tanks hanging high on the wall and a long chain to pull that released the water to flush the toilet. We were all amazed by this mechanical marvel and would pull every chain in the restroom. We also saw steam radiators for the first time. We learned that we must use the urinals and not urinate on the hot radiator in the restroom. One of my classmates was a slow learner and soon got caught. For his punishment he had to stay after school and print fifty times, "I will not wet on the radiator."

Our parents were involved in our education and visited school several times a year and came to P.T.A., school plays, and other events. We also had to take all of our completed papers home so that our parents could see how good or bad we were doing. Our teachers glued little paper stars on our attendance sheets for being on time and for keeping our hands and nails clean. School was the first experience we had in being competitive and where someone other than family was interested in our work or hygiene.

Mom (2nd row, 4th from left) grade school, about 1917. Teacher McKinley.

There were three buildings on the school grounds. The Old Rock School was boarded up, and we were restricted from entering it. It did house the school bell which was usually rung by the janitor or one of the teachers. The red brick grade school building was just east of the rock building. (This building has since been torn down.) The high school building was across the grass, north of the rock building. I went to the first, second, and third grades in the red brick building, and my fifth grade classes were in the high school building.

The only extracurricular activities were boys' basketball and the school band. The boys' basketball team competed with several schools in the other small towns in the Gunnison area and I remember that we always had a winning team. The band was composed of both high school girls and boys, who played at the basketball games and marched in many of the town parades. Most of the high school students learned to play an instrument and were members of the band.

CHURCH

There were two churches in Crested Butte; the Union Congregational (Protestant), and St. Patrick's Church (Catholic). I didn't know very much about the Protestant Church because as youngsters we were forbidden under the threat of sin, to go to a church other than Catholic. The Protestant Church didn't have a fulltime minister but one came from Gunnison to hold Sunday services. Services were always later in the day than the Catholic Mass.

St. Patrick's Church had a large number of parishioners, as the majority of the families in Crested Butte were Catholic, and a full time priest who lived in a house just east of the church. Mass was celebrated every morning of the week and was over in time for school. There were always two Masses on Sunday. The second Mass was a High Mass sung in Latin by the Priest and with a lot of additional ritual. It seemed quite long, so I always tried to go the early Mass.

During the week on some evenings there were also special services like the recitation of the Rosary or the Stations of the Cross. In all cases, all of the prayers were said aloud.

Most babies were christened in the Catholic Church shortly after they were born. A christening was always a very joyous affair. My cousin Jouette and I were christened on the same day. Jouette's parents, Uncle Joe and Aunt Rose Starika were my sponsors, and my Mom and Dad were hers. After the ceremony, a dinner and dance was held at the Kochevar house. All of our relatives and friends attended. Uncle Joe Starika played the accordion for the dance.

The sacrament of Baptism was the beginning of your Catholic faith. Through the rest of your life you would partake in First Holy Communion, Confession, Confirmation, Matrimony, and at the end of life, the final sacrament, Extreme Unction. If you became a priest you celebrated the sacrament of Holy Orders.

For one month during the summer we had vacation school, Catechism classes, held at the Church by Benedictine Sisters. Sisters Gabrielle, and Laura were from Chicago, and Sister Marian was from Canyon City, Colorado. We were taught about the Catholic religion and prepared for our First Holy Communion. The older children who had completed their communion prepared for Confirmation. These classes were attended by almost every Catholic child in town and by a few non-Catholics. They were fun, and we were always rewarded with a Holy Picture, medal or statue for good work and perfect attendance.

The Saturday before our First Holy Communion there was a class picnic that everyone looked forward to. It was usually held at the Smith Hill Campground. Early the morning of the picnic we would all meet in front of the Church with a sack lunch and start our long walk down First Street passed Peanut Mine up railroad spur to the Smith Hill Campground. The distance was several miles and the younger children were tended to and helped by the older children. It must have been a difficult walk for the Sisters who were in full habit but no one seemed to mind as we all took our time and sang songs that were led by the Sisters.

Finally arriving at the picnic site along Slate River we removed our shoes and stockings and waded across a shallow portion of the river to our planned picnic spot. We fished and played games. Again Holy pictures and medals were the prizes. We also had free time to explore the area and some of the bravest boys stripped to their under shorts and swam in the cold water. After an exhausting but joyful day, we started the long walk back to Saint Patrick's Church, which always seemed much longer than trip to get to the campground. I don't think anyone had a problem sleeping that night.

The next day was the day for which we had been preparing and anticipating. It was the day many of us would receive our First Communion or our Confirmation. I made my First Communion the summer of 1939. The Sisters had worked hard and prepared us well. For four weeks we were taught the importance and the significance of this day. We all had our first Confession, and now we were going to receive Christ for the first time. Walking to the altar, we were afraid but also happy as our proud parents and relatives watched us walk to and from the altar. This was again a time for celebration.

Again, I shared this day with my cousin Jouette who also received her First Communion. We had a great dinner and party at the Kochevar house with friends and relatives joining us in the celebration.

After this momentous day, I, like most of my friends, went to confession every Saturday. We didn't have much to confess but we went anyway. A typical confession was "Bless me Father for I have sinned. My last Confession was a week ago. I told two lies, I said a dirty word three times, and I disobeyed my parents three times." For this my penance was three Hail Marys.

The priest and I then prayed the Act of Contrition and I went to a pew and prayed the Hail Marys. We youngsters weren't the only Catholics to go to Confession every Saturday. Several of the elderly women and a couple of men did also. I couldn't imagine what these women and men did during the week that required them to go to Confession every Saturday. These folks, our grandmothers particularly, never missed a daily Mass after which they would get together in little groups and talk. If it was really cold out, they stayed in the rear of the church and when it was warmer they would talk on the street corner near the City Hall. I am not sure what they talked about, but they always talked. We could see them still talking and waving their hands when we were on our way to school.

They could not talk to their neighbor over the clothesline in Crested Butte. Because of the deep snow in winter, to hang clothes the women stood on an elevated platform, often off of a porch or back door and pinned their clothes to a wire, which was reeled out on a pulley to a tall pole several yards away.

When I was about nine or ten years old, I decided that I wanted to be an altar boy and assist the priest in the preparation and celebration of Mass. Some of the responsibilities for an altar boy were filling the cruets with wine and water, assisting the priest in donning his vestments, and lighting the candles on and around the altar. We were also responsible for ringing the church bell, which reminded the congregation that it was time for services. I think we rang the bell thirty minutes before Mass and the last bell just before the service began.

Vacation school picnic, 1942.

BELOW LEFT: *First Holy Communion, 1939.*
BELOW RIGHT: *Altar Boy (the writer).*

Like the priest, altar boys had special vestments for particular Masses but usually not as ornate as the priest's. We had three cassocks, each a different color --- red, white, and black. Over the red or black cassock we wore a white lace surplice. With the white cassock, worn only on very special days like Easter, we wore a red stole trimmed with gold and a matching sash. The red cassock was worn most of the time, but during Lent and Masses for the Dead, Black was worn.

At St. Patrick's Church we had about eight to twelve altar boys. The priest always had at least two boys to assist him with Mass every morning and twice on Sundays, and Rosary a couple of evenings each week. During Lent the Stations of the Cross were added to the evening schedule. With this busy schedule of services we altar boys spent several hours a week in church.

The Mass was recited in Latin and we answered the priest's prayers in Latin. Most of our responses were short and easy to recall but there were a couple longer ones that were harder memorize. We had prayer cards on the kneeler, which we could refer to if necessary. I think I needed the cards every time I had to recite the Confiteor.

CHAPTER 10: HOLIDAYS

After talking about religion and church, it is so easy to relate to the holidays we enjoyed in Crested Butte.

CHRISTMAS

The Christmas holiday season started on the eve of the sixth of December on Saint Nicholas Day, and lasted until after the January 6th, All King's Day. Most of the families celebrating Christmas went to the woods before the sixth of December to cut an evergreen to bring home to decorate.

I think the tree at Grandma and Grandpa Kochevar's was the one all of the family remembered the best. The saloon had very high ceilings, and the tree was always over eight feet tall. It was always placed on a table in the northeast corner of the saloon and the angel at the top of it looked like it was reaching for the sky.

The Christmas tree lights were assembled in a series circuit. If one light in the series would burn out, all of the lights would loose power so you would have to remove and replace every light until you found the bad one. Needless to say, you spent considerable time checking lights if you wanted to keep the tree bright.

After we encircled the tree with lights, glass balls and other decorations were hung. Next we put angel hair around the lights which gave them a special glow. Last we placed metal tinsel on each branch, one strand at a time. Decorating the tree was a family affair.

In Europe, December 6th, Saint Nicholas (Santa Claus) Day, was the day everyone received gifts. Being in America, we had the best of both continents receiving gifts on Saint Nicholas Day and Christmas day. On the evening of the fifth of December, we would put our caps on the table and leave the tree lights on so Saint Nicholas could find our house. He would bring candy and fruit if we were good and a piece of coal or a rotten potato if we were bad.

My sisters always got candy, but one year when I went to my cap, I found both a chunk of coal and an old potato. I was in tears when Mom and Dad directed me to the coal bucket to dispense with my chunk of coal. Near to it I found that Saint Nick had hid my candy and fruit. I think Saint Nicholas was telling me something.

Around this same time the town of Crested Butte placed a large Christmas tree in the ground in the center of the main street at the intersection of Elk and Third Streets and decorated it with large lights. The tree was cut in the mountains and drug by horses over the snow, set up and decorated by the volunteer fire department. Many of the townspeople and most of the kids waited on the street until the firemen threw the switch to light the tree.

Christmas was a great day for everyone, especially the kids. It started off with Midnight Mass celebrated on Christmas Eve. I can remember getting up in the middle of the night, getting dressed, leaving the warm house, and walking to church in the snow. I don't think Mom and Dad even went to bed. They were too busy preparing everything for Christmas Day. I always checked under the tree before we left for Mass to see if Santa had come to the house while I was asleep. He never did.

Mom and I went to Mass while Dad stayed home with my little sister, Carol Ann. Staying awake in the church was very difficult, but Mom gently nudged me several times. After Mass everyone was in very good spirits, and stood around shaking hands and wishing each other a Merry Christmas. I kept tugging on Mom. I was anxious to get home and see if Santa made it to the house while we were in church. Finally we walked rather briskly back to the house and Dad met us at the door with a Merry Christmas.

I pulled off my cap, coat, and boots and ran to the tree. Santa had come while I was away. Mom and Dad let me open one present before I went back to bed but the rest would wait unit morning when my little sister woke up.

I was up early and made sure Carol Ann was out of bed early also. After opening all of my presents and having a great morning, I met with my cousins and friends and we went house to house wishing everyone a Merry Christmas. It was like trick or treat during Halloween, and almost everyone gave us a piece of candy or a penny. Some families even gave us a nickel. We also went to every saloon in town to wish the owner a Merry Christmas and he gave us candy bars. After good wishes to almost everyone in Crested Butte, we returned to a large family dinner at Grandma and Grandpa Kochevar's. Total attendance at dinner was near twenty. There was not enough room at the main table so us kids all sat at separate tables. I don't think Grandma and Mom ever ate at the table, as they were busy preparing and serving the food to all of us. They didn't go hungry, though, as they frequently tasted the food to make sure it was done just right.

New Year's Day (the Feast of the Circumcision) to us kids was just like any other Sunday, and we went to Mass in the morning. For the adults, the night before was a real celebration. There was a New Year's Eve dance in town that most of them attended. At midnight, the New Year was brought in with jubilation and lots of noise. The church bells would ring, the siren at City Hall would sound, and many of the men would fire several rounds from their rifle into the air. One year some of the men in town set off several sticks of dynamite on Chocolate Peak. Not only did the noise of the blast awaken everyone in town it also broke several windows. I don't think anyone confessed to setting off the dynamite, but everyone had an idea who the culprits were.

The Christmas season ended with All Kings Day (the Feast of the Epiphany) on January 6. After this day, everyone took the trimmings off their trees and placed them into boxes to be used the following year. The trees was then taken outside and hauled away. After thirty some days of standing inside, there were often more pine needles on the floor than there were on the tree.

EASTER

Another long holiday season was Easter. It started with Ash Wednesday, the first day of lent, and ended forty days later on Easter Sunday. On the morning of Ash Wednesday we all went to Mass and the priest made a cross on your forehead with ashes. You could distinguish the non-Catholics from the Catholics that day. The non-Catholics were the ones without the black ash smudge on their foreheads. Lent was also a time of sorrow and penance and it was customary for every Catholic to give up something he enjoyed, as a penance. Many kids gave up candy for this 40-day period. During lent the priest wore black vestments, as did the altar boys and there was no music in Church. There were also church services every night and Stations of the Cross.

The Sunday before Easter was Palm Sunday (Passion Sunday), the day the people of Jerusalem proclaimed Christ as their King. The priest blessed palms and gave each person a palm leaf to take home. The palms were displayed in the home near a crucifix or other religious object for the rest of the year. Mom always braided our palm leaves together before she hung them.

The Friday following Palm Sunday was Good Friday, the day Christ was crucified and hung on the cross. For Catholics, this was the saddest day of the year. It was a day of fasting for adults and abstinence from meat for all of us. When I was growing up in Crested Butte all Fridays were days of abstinence from meat. On Good Friday we were also told we couldn't dig in the ground. This was marble season, but we were not allowed to scribe a line on the ground. If we were planned to play marbles on that day, we played on the sidewalk and marked the surface with a piece of chalk.

Easter Sunday (the Resurrection) was a happy day as Christ had risen from the dead. The day started with a joyous Mass, with priest and altar boys in white and decorated vestments, music and beautiful spring flowers decorating the altar. When we got home we exchanged and hunted for colorfully decorated eggs that the Easter bunny had brought and hidden. The eggs and the Easter bunny signified New Life. This was also the end of Lent, and we no longer had to continue the penance we had imposed on ourselves on Ash Wednesday.

MAY DAY

The first of May was May Day and to celebrate all of the grade school children made May baskets out of colored paper decorated with crayons or different colored paper and filled them with wild flowers to give to our parents. The wild flowers were found and picked in a field near the school. If a variety of flowers could not be found in abundance, we could always fill the basket with dandelion flowers.

MEMORIAL DAY

Memorial Day was founded after the Civil War to honor the soldiers from the North who were killed in that war. Subsequently it included the men killed in all wars and was also a day to commemorate all who passed before us. Early morning on this day we cleaned and decorated all of the graves of our deceased relatives and friends followed by a large parade, which was led by the men, and women who had served our Country. Behind the military contingent were members of the lodges, townspeople and all of the children. Services were held at the cemetery and afterwards there was a luncheon and dance at the Croation Hall. A military parade from the town of Crested Butte to the cemetery is still customary to this date.

FOURTH OF JULY

Fourth of July, Independence Day, was celebrated with a parade down Main Street of local organizations, the High School Band, and anyone who wanted to join in. After the parade it was time for a picnic, either a fish fry near Almont or a barbecue (Pachinka) at the Gothic campground. For the Pachinka a few men would start early in the morning preparing the barbecue pit and nursing a hot bed of coals in the bottom of it to roast a lamb or goat. The women organized in groups preparing all of the other foods necessary for the large dinner. We kids romped in the woods, fished, and played games. There was always plenty of beer, soda pop, and accordion music near the site of the barbecue. Dinner was truly delicious. In the evening we returned to town to fire off our skyrockets and the firecrackers. During those years fireworks were limited because of the war and town did not have a fireworks display.

ABOVE: Boys – Jay Naglich and the writer. Grown-ups – Joe Tezak, Nick Naglich, Barbara Naglich, Dad, and Lorenz Naglich. Picture taken about 1938.

HALLOWEEN

Halloween for the grade school kids was much like the Halloween of today. There weren't the elaborate costumes that you see today but the idea of going house to house shouting, "trick or treat," and receiving candy was the same. Halloween wasn't only for the young kids in Crested Butte. The older kids, boys mainly, did a lot of tricking but no treating. They waxed and soaped all of the car and house windows they could get to and turned over several outhouses. One year they turned over one of the outhouses when it was occupied. The tenant wasn't hurt but he wasn't a happy man. This was the busiest night of the year for the local town Marshall.

CHAPTER 11:
OUR DAILY BREAD

While writing about the holidays, I couldn't keep my mind from drifting to the many different and delicious foods we ate. This chapter is also a tasty and fitting way to end the many words I have put together about our family and our life in Crested Butte.

Breakfast was always a large meal but usually served in shifts because the men went to work very early, the women and children went to church and then the older children went to school. Other than church, the women seemed to spend the whole day in the kitchen. Lunch was simple, leftovers, sandwiches, or just homemade bread with butter and an apple. The evening meal was a large meal, and the family always shared it together.

Of the few ethnic breakfasts that I remember, my favorite was *starec*. *Starec* is made mainly with eggs, milk and flour. The mixture is then sauteed in a skillet and chopped into little crumbles similar to scrambled eggs. The big difference is that it is then eaten by taking a spoonful of it and dipping it into coffee that was sweetened with sugar and cream. Sound good? It was!

Another Slovenian breakfast dish was *zulica*. *Zulica* was cut up pigs feet boiled in water with some spices for several hours. When the boiling was completed it was divided into several bowls and set in a cool place to gel. The following morning this rare treat was eaten with fresh horseradish from the garden.

Our neighbor across the street from us was of Mexican heritage. On Saturday mornings I liked to invite myself to Johnny Martinez's house for breakfast as his Mother always made flour tortillas that day. She would mix the dough, flatten it and brown the tortilla on the very hot stovetop. Covered with butter while still hot it was another special treat.

Uncle Martin (Teenie) Tezak had the same non-ethnic breakfast every morning. He could buy his breakfast ingredients in any grocery store in town. Uncle Teenie always had several wieners boiling on the stove. Dad and I would visit on Sunday morning and have a boiled wiener dipped in ketchup, fresh bread and a cup of coffee.

There were few refrigerators in town, so smoking meat was a great way to preserve it. In the fall, the family would get together and butcher a hog. I don't think any part of the hog was wasted. Most of the meat was cut and hung in a tall tin smokehouse where the meats would be seasoned by a sweet wood smoke from the slow burning fire on its floor. Hams, chops, *klobasi*, and other meats were smoked. *Klobasi* was a sausage made from lean ground pork, garlic and spices with the casings made from the intestines from the hog that were cleaned and soaked until used. Blood sausage was made with the blood of the hog mixed with soaked rice and spices. It was not smoked but baked in the oven until crisp and eaten as a breakfast treat. The fat of the hog was melted over a hot fire and rendered into lard. The meats skimmed from the melted fat, cracklings or *ocferka* were spread on fresh bread and were best served while still hot.

At large family gatherings, every relative had their specialties. Smoked meats or *klobasi* with homemade sauerkraut or sour turnips were always a main dish. Aunt Margaret Kochevar's parents came to Crested Butte from Northern Italy and she often prepared a dish called *consace*. This was like a meat ravioli that was baked in butter and sprinkled with a coarse goat cheese. There were never any leftovers, and Aunt Margaret took only her cleaned platter back home.

Mom used to make a dish the family really enjoyed. It was a cornmeal mush called *zganci*. The Italians had a similar dish called *polenta*. Stewed kidneys in heavy brown gravy were usually served on top of it.

Yet another Slovenian dish I remember was *struklje*. *Struklje* was a side dish made by scattering fried and scrambled egg onto noodle dough, which was then rolled, sliced and boiled like a dumpling.

Besides the meats, vegetables and other main dishes, the breads and pastries were scrumptious and took a very long time to prepare. Because of this painstaking work, these pastries were usually made only for special occasions. The most notable were *potica* and *strudel*.

Mom's *potica* was made with a sweet bread dough that after rising was rolled and pulled thin, covered with a mixture of walnuts, honey or sugar, eggs and cinnamon rolled, left to rise again and baked. Her *strudel* was remarkable. The dough was stretched and pulled by her nimble fingers until it was as thin as parchment paper. Then it was usually dappled with apples, cinnamon and butter, rolled, fitted into a baking pan and baked to a rich golden brown. My Mother was the "strudel lady." Later in her life she made strudels for all of her children, family, friends and anyone who asked her for one or did her a favor. In 1991 Mom made over100 apple strudels. Most of them were made from the old apple tree just west of the house. Mom had to share the apples with the local bird population that would peck at the apples as soon as they were ripe.

Mom used to make an Italian cookie called a *pizzelle*, which was as wafer made with an iron similar to a waffle iron. The result was a delicate, thin, beautifully patterned crisp cookie. She, also, made Pohanje, which was sis Mose's favorite. It is a Slovenian pastry made from dough rolled thin and cut into three-inch diamond shapes, deep fried, drained on paper and sprinkled with powdered sugar.

My sisters and their daughters still make apple strudel and walnut poticas for special occasions. I don't know anyone who still makes the other ethnic foods I wrote about in this chapter.

I often wonder if all of these foods could possibly taste as good as I remember them.

Thomas Wolfe in his book, *You Can't Go Home Again,* emphasized that everything changes and nothing remains the same. Even if you are gone for just an hour, things have changed. He was certainly right about Crested Butte. Once the mines and railroad closed in 1952, most of the people left Crested Butte and went to work at the CF&I coal mines in Trinidad, the Steel Mill in Pueblo or other places where they could find employment. Out of necessity, they sold their homes in Crested Butte for next to nothing. Years later the new immigrants arrived. They were not the laborers but the opportunists and entrepreneurs, who saw the beauty of the valley and the majestic mountains and wished to capitalize on them. Crested Butte is now a tourist Mecca with a ski resort, golf course, hotels, condos, various tourist attractions and luxury homes. These homes are scattered on the majestic mountains as ornaments on a Christmas tree, but they don't detract from the real beauty in my memory of Avalon.

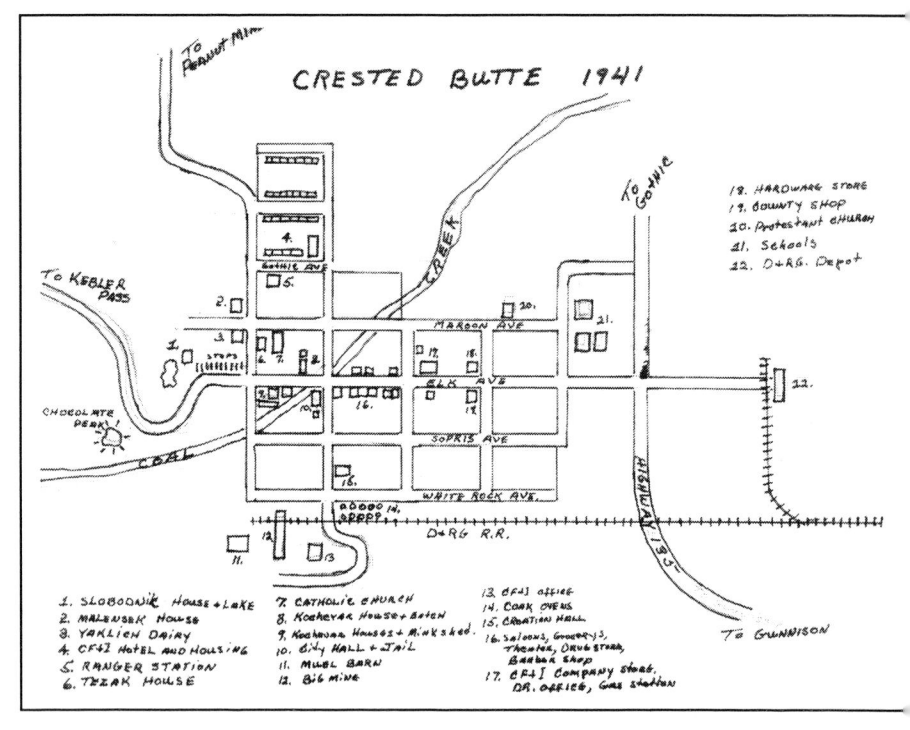

Crested Butte town map.